IN THIS EARTH
&
IN THAT WIND

Royal Asiatic Society, Korea Branch
Handbook Series, Number 2

in
this
earth
&
in
that
wind
this is Korea

BY LEE O-YOUNG
TRANSLATED BY DAVID I. STEINBERG
ILLUSTRATED BY BAE YOONG

PUBLISHED FOR RAS-KB
BY SEOUL COMPUTER PRESS

IN THIS EARTH
&
IN THAT WIND:
This is Korea

Lee O-Young
Translated by David I. Steinberg
Illustrated by Bae Yoong

Copyright 1967 by Royal Asiatic Society,
Korea Branch, Box 255, CPO, Seoul, Korea

Second Printing 1983

Published for RAS-KB by Seoul Computer Press
Registration No. 15-21
CPO Box 8850, Tel. 261-6566

Library of Congress Catalog Card Number:
67-31380

Layout: Sandra Mattielli

Printed in Korea

CONTENTS

To
my wife,
Ann Myongsook Lee

D.I.S.

The subjective impression is for the writer
what experimentation is for the scientist,
but with this difference, that with the scientist
the work of the intelligence precedes, and with the writer
it comes afterwards. Anything we have not had to decipher
and clarify by our own personal effort,
anything that was clear before we intervened,
is not our own.

Proust: *The Past Recaptured*

TRANSLATOR'S PREFACE

The Setting

TRADITIONAL societies in many parts of Asia have been undergoing a process of rapid, although somewhat amorphous, social change. Specific changes may differ from society to society, and although some general patterns do emerge, the process itself is often confusing, frustrating and even terrifying both to the members of that society and it's observers. The traditional values which have been the cement of these societies for centuries have been eroded by the introduction of new ideas from abroad. Some of these ideas may perhaps be directly pertinent to the stated goals of the nation as expressed by its leaders, and others may be by-products spread through a concensus of its intellectuals or people.

It has also become obvious that change is ubiquitous

and cannot be easily controlled. Factories may mean adaptation to new working habits and to a new concept of time. Paternalism in business and industry often cannot meet the demands of competition on the world market. Urbanization usually introduces smaller housing units destructive to the traditional or extended family system. Modern education for youth and their increasing ability to find employment commensurate with their education and qualifications, based upon performance rather than familial ties, tend to lessen these ties and produce individualism with widespread and important social, economic and political implications. These few examples are of phenomena so various that academicians have written scores of books on them. These changes are merely small patterns in the complex quilt which has been called cultural change.

All societies are attempting to change in some degree and manner and the slogans extolling such progress may be useful but they are rarely sufficient. It is not enough simply to know what you want to change into. A period of cultural change in any society calls for intense, serious and sensitive efforts to try to come to grips with the traditional society so you know what you are changing from. Understanding the modernization process postulates that you know where you have been; only then can you know where you are going. But not everyone necessarily wants to go in the same direction at the same speed. Instead of one homogeneous society there may be several different blurred groups with invisible margins. Societies then lose their coherence and individuals their confidence in themselves and their direction. One can no longer unquestioningly accept a certain course of action as adequate simply because it has worked in the past. Conflicts between generations are a natural consequence.

Then, for the first time perhaps, some of the intellectuals in that society, both young and old, become concerned with the fabric of their traditional society, with its complex of values, norms and attitudes. They are no longer content to know how to operate within that society, something which they had always done unconsciously; but they may have become interested in going beyond the outward manifestations of that society to discover how it works, why it has evolved into the form it has come to take, and they may question whether it has indeed been the best of all possible worlds. Some may become convinced that not all modernization or change is good, and not all that is traditional is bad. This attitude may be a part of a complex reaction to overwhelming foreign influences often associated with nationalism.

So the paradox is that a searching re-evaluation may be made of a traditional culture as a result of the process of modernization. While many may realize that much of importance can be learned from abroad, they may also begin to consider which of their own traditional values are relevant to their goals. They may begin to be selective in trying to choose and reject certain of their inheritances.

Of course, cultural change is not so simple. We have learned through a variety of unexpected experiences that we cannot pick and choose areas of change or tradition as we would fruit in a supermarket. Even with the sophisticated social science methodology and psychological testing we have today, governments have often been surprised with the changes that they have induced and many have reaped the whirlwind.

But self-scrutiny is not the only type of analysis taking place in these societies. Foreign, largely Western, observers have been trying for centuries to draw portraits of these "strange and distant" lands. Many of the books, monographs, journals and articles produced by them are descriptive studies mirroring the prejudices of the age in which they were written and the society from which the author came. Some contain useful material even today. Often we wish to look back at a foreign society and explore something which now seems terribly important to us but which a hundred years ago seemed unimportant to the people of that culture. So the observations of foreigners about the cultures of Asia have had a distinct usefulness, a fresh perspective.

The dialogue between Asians and Westerners has in general grown as more Asians write and think about their own societies, as more foreigners have first-hand knowledge about Asia and as Asian studies are more and more taught in the schools and colleges of the West. But in some societies this dialogue is really just beginning. Korea is one such case.

As part of the "Great Tradition" of East Asia, Korea has shared with her more powerful neighbor, China, the Confucian tradition for scholarship, learning and the life of the literati. It has been a proud tradition, one that can take its place among the most important civilizing influences in world history. It has placed the scholar at the pinnacle of prestige and success in Korean society. It has given intellectual interests paramountcy.

But this tradition did not encourage speculation on the

nature of this society, outside of the accepted court-centered Confucian preconceptions, until the close of the nineteenth century when, alas, it was too late. The Japanese occupation which lasted thirty-six years did not encourage it. The Korean War of 1950–53 disrupted all academic pursuits. Thus only in recent years has there been the opportunity for Korean scholars to have the interest and leisure, together with exposure to other cultures through literature and personal experience, to consider the nature of their traditional society and the changes which have taken place in it.

Foreign scholars have been no better off. Korea was the "Hermit Kingdom" until the close of the nineteenth century, and the Japanese occupation which followed severely retarded the development of Western scholarship on Korea. True, a few missionaries had a profound understanding of aspects of Korean history and society, but their interests were in large part parochial.

Korea was also overwhelmed by the importance of her larger neighbors. China has always had a fascination and attraction for the Asian specialist, and if one is to study East Asia, why not study it at its source, China? The rapid modernization and industrial growth of Japan attracted wide interest among Western scholars. Virtually all attention was given to China and Japan, while Korea was ignored. It has only been lately that Korea has become a focus in the academic community for and of itself.

Thus the dialogue on Korean cultural change is just beginning.

In order that this dialogue continues and grows, there is need for a variety of research and publications which will contribute to the growing interchange of knowledge and materials between Korea and the foreign community. There is an urgent need for more academic works by Koreans and foreigners in Western languages. Korean scholars must play their proper role among the ever-increasing community of international social scientists. More Koreans and foreigners have been doing field research and publishing the results in a variety of international journals. The prospects of eliminating the paucity of materials on Korea are quite good and growing better each year. But is this sufficient? Are there not other needs? While the academic specialist requires material full of statistically valid data based on proper sampling techniques, there is also a need for intuitive insight and imagination about the nature of society. Indeed, there is also a need for poetry and speculation. Even poetic error may reveal as much as it may mislead.

Practically, the visitor and the resident in Korea need to have resource materials with which to understand this society better. Very few such materials on Korea exist today. This present volume is in the nature of an attempt to enhance the dialogue so recently begun. It was written to help explain traditional Korea to the Koreans. It was translated to help explain Korea to the foreign community.

The Book

The publication of *In This Earth and In That Wind* in book form in Korean took place in December, 1963 and was an attempt by a young Korean intellectual to think about his society with imagination and insight. The original articles were first published serially in the *Kyong-hyang Shinmun*, a Korean language daily in Seoul. Since the first edition of the book appeared, there have been nineteen printings. It has affected a whole generation of young people who have responded to the concepts and ideas presented in it. The volume has probably had a wider readership than any other single volume of its kind in recent Korean literary history. It has been praised and disputed but it must have provided its Korean readers with some additional insight and understanding about their own society to attract such wide readership.

The work, as first published, was composed of three parts: 1) "In This Earth and In That Wind"; 2) "A Melancholy Sketchbook"; and 3) "Undercurrents of Korean Literature." The first section, the bulk of the book, is composed of fifty separate yet related essays; it is this section that is translated here.

The purpose of each of these fifty essays is not to present a complete and detailed picture of Korean society. Rather, the author has attempted to take the commonplace in Korean life—which everyone resident in Korea, both Korean and foreigner, has seen or felt—and draw from these daily habits, customs or items a picture of Korean society. He often contrasts aspects of Korean culture with that of foreign nations and draws a variety of conclusions about the nature of Korean society from these contrasts. The author has done this with a sensitivity which is remarkable and which, in the translator's knowledge, has never been presented before in English. He has been able to see beyond outward manifestations into something more complex. He has explained to Korean and foreign readers alike something more of Korea.

These essays do not attempt to be definitive and should not be so interpreted. They are not supported by social science data which can be verfied. They were written in a conversational style of Korean, rather informally. Yet each one offers to the reader some new concept, a different perspective, a penetrating idea which can be the subject for reflection. These essays are thus in a sense poetical—they are composed of insights and glimpses beyond reality on which the reader will be able to expand and through which he may wish to reconsider the nature of his experience in Korea. The essays therefore are often controversial. If they were not, they would have little value. The ideas presented are points of view from which further discussion will naturally be evoked.

The author, in these essays, is essentially concerned with traditional Korea—a Korea which, though in the process of change, still retains many of the characteristics of a traditional society. As an intellectual, he often questions certain Korean customs, and the reader who has had experience in Korea will realize that many of these customs are evolving. Thus it is important to stress that the reader should not read only this book if he wishes to learn about Korea. It should be taken within a broader context. It must be a sauce, not the main course.

I owe to the reader an explanation of how this translation came to be written. For some time during my five-year residence in Korea I had been concerned that my study of the Korean language had been limited to the dialogues presented to the foreigner in the textbooks on Korean, all of which were very limited and linguistically rather than culturally oriented. After experimentation with a play or two, I searched for a work which would afford me an opportunity to improve my reading of Korean and which would also assist me in better understanding the society in which I was resident.

At first I began this translation as a language exercise for my own amusement. I had been asked to write articles on my impressions of Korea for *The Korea Times,* the English-language Seoul daily. I felt at that time that it was presumptuous for me to do so, and at the same time I began to question the literature which was being produced for foreign consumption on aspects of Korean life. I was worried that the articles I had seen written by foreigners on Korea were often polarized; too many praised aspects of Korean life which many Koreans felt were questionable; others were too critical of a nation they did not understand. One could never be sure of the motivations of non-academic foreigners writing on Korea. So too, one was uncertain about the motives of Koreans writing in English for foreign consumption. Some said those things which they thought foreigners wanted to hear, some were nationalistic, some self-deprecatory. I became more interested in what Koreans wrote about themselves for internal consumption, those works written without the thought that they would find their way into foreign hands. I hoped that by finding a work which had been widely read by Koreans perhaps I would be able to discover what Koreans thought about their own society. These translations, which began as language study, began appearing weekly in *The Korea Times* on November 16, 1966.

I have taken the liberty of editing some of these translations in order to make them more understandable to the foreign reader. Notes and footnotes have been provided by the translator unless otherwise indicated. In many cases the author has written extensive notes for the Korean reader, but when these have explained Western societies or have delved into Korean history to a degree to which the average reader of this book might not be interested, these have been eliminated. Where appropriate, some notes have been incorporated into the body of the text.

Korean names have been given in their Korean order, with the surname first. Romanization has followed the McCune-Reischauer system first promulgated in the *Transactions of the Korea Branch of the Royal Asiatic Society* in 1939. Exceptions in both stylistic patterns have been made when common usage has made it desirable, such as in the spelling of Syngman Rhee. Chinese names follow the same order as the Korean, and the Wade-Giles romanization has been used for them.

It is hoped that this volume will be of help to the foreigners resident in Korea and to those abroad interested in Korea and her unique culture. I have tried to keep the translations close to the original Korean, as far as practicable, as some of them have found their way into the hands of Korean students of English who use them for study purposes since most of them are acquainted with the Korean text.

This translation does not pretend to be a scholarly work. It is an effort to provide another glimpse of Korea from an unusual vantagepoint. I have learned a great deal about Korea from preparing this translation and I hope that it will be of assistance to those who wish to think a little more deeply about life in Korea.

It would be virtually impossible to thank all of the friends and colleagues who have assisted me in this work. I should like to mention the assistance and patience of my Korean teacher, Mr. Sohn Han, who has been kind and understanding throughout. Without the advice of the author, Mr. Lee O-young, and his assistance, the work could not have been undertaken. Mr. Lee Kyu-hyun, former Editor of *The Korea Times,* encouraged me throughout my attempt. I would like to thank the members of the Council of the Korea Branch of the Royal Asiatic Society who have proded me to put these translations into book form and who have sponsored this publication. I would also like to thank Dr. Peter Lee of the University of Hawaii for his corrections and criticism.

To my secretaries, Mr. Lee Eui-kwan, Miss Han Sung-lim and Miss Bang Sun-sook, go my grateful thanks for typing innumerable drafts and finished copies far beyond the call of duty.

The greatest debt of any man is perhaps to his wife. Ann Myongsook Lee encouraged and cajoled me all along the way, corrected my innumerable errors and illuminated a myriad of obscurities. It may be truly said that without her this book would not exist.

David I. Steinberg
December, 1967
Seoul, Korea

IN THIS EARTH
&
IN THAT WIND

Bae yoons 67

Introduction

1. Behind the Landscape

IT was a county road not even on maps; a road which can be seen in any rural part of Korea if you go a little off any national highway; loess earth, gravel, and here and there white plantains were in bloom. The road that winds along the base of the mountain extended, tracing a lonely curve without a human sign. Country people usually call it a "cart track."

I drove along that road in a jeep. Through the windshield, a little more than two spans, I was looking at my homeland; my village, the same as ever, common, constrained, solitary and impoverished; a landscape buried as it has been for many years in the blankness of oblivion. It was a still and simple landscape of broken thatch roofs, stone walls, broken stone tablets along a stream lined by poplars, the Confucian study hall, abandoned graves with their grass plots, accacia, and barley fields.

There was a stillness like the beating of an egret's wings, a ripple in a pool, a withered leaf falling, a shadowed valley. But it was akin to the stillness around a ruin, a stillness neither to be understood nor wholly explained simply as nostalgia. A lazy sorrow and drowzy stagnation gaped like a void or a deep wound, a sort of pain rather than beauty. Without looking into that void or wound, you cannot truly understand the weak-colored landscape stretching out there.

You cannot feel this without seeing the swollen stomachs of the village children, without smelling the sweat of the rural wives with their gaunt cheekbones, and without hearing their songs and their way of speaking nonchalantly to one another.

As the jeep turned a corner on an eroded hill and began to go down I saw all these things. Although it happens too often and is too trifling to be called an incident, it penetrated my mind with strong impressions.

In front walked an old couple. Although they were frightened by the sound of the horn and rushed to try to escape, they seemed to be too frightened. They suddenly grasped each other's hands and awkwardly ran in front of the car without stopping; and then, as their rubber shoes had fallen off, they stumbled backward to pick them up. The car almost ran them over. This is the whole story of what happened then. It was in sight only for a few tens of seconds and the car again sped on leaving them behind as if nothing had happened.

The driver first laughed at their folly and then got angry, but that also was over in a moment. He drove on expressionless, but I remembered everything exactly, and the image did not easily disappear.

Their faces, suntanned and full of blistered freckles, the fearful and upset expression, and the contour of their backs as they fled like staggering animals; two withered hands tightly clasping each other without wanting to let go even in that emergency, one hand holding a bag with dried haddock sticking out, one hand intending to pick up a pair of rubber shoes . . . trembling hands. . . .

I have seen Koreans. I have encountered the image of my ancestors who have lived that way for a thousand years; the image of the chased! That image was not as refined as that of a foreigner who leisurely escapes from a car on an asphalt road. Like the driver's meaningless laughter, their fleeting images reminded me of a flock of ducks and chickens on the roadside as they run away, with the flapping of wings, in front of a speeding car.

When misfortune, poverty and tyranny, and so many unexpected disasters assailed them without warning, did they have to be chased away with the gestures of animals? Did they have to escape with such an expression and such trembling hands?

Our secret and our hearts are in this atmosphere; in this earth and in that wind which is so like the color of our skin.

Bae Young 67

2. On Crying

With cry and moan
The birds fly overhead.
Tremendous sorrow nests in me
And cries and moans after I wake.[1]

LIKE these lines from the Koryŏ Dynasty "Song of Green Mountain," there are those who, whenever they wake up, spend the day in crying and tears. In sorrow they cry, in hunger they cry, and in grievance they cry. Even when they are merry they cry because they are happy. Although the American Sioux Indians are known to be a people who cry easily, they can never equal our Korean people.

One cannot speak of Korea without mentioning cry-

---

1. *Anthology of Korean Poetry*, compiled and translated by Peter H. Lee (New York: John Day Co., 1964).

4

ing and tears. Not only do we cry but we hear everything as crying. It all begins with the word "to cry." When we hear any sound, we automatically call it "crying." We translate the English "birds sing" as "birds cry." Although "sing" means to sing a song, we express it as crying because even the same bird sounds which Westerners hear as a merry song, we hear as sad crying. Even the Chinese, another Oriental people, strictly distinguish between the word 鳴 (a bird call), 啼 (to twitter or chirp) and 泣 (to weep silent tears). But we even say that the sound of bells is crying and that the sound of rice paper rustling in the wind on the edge of a Korean door is also crying.

In the following poem it is written, "In the bedroom the lighted candle burns. From whom is it separated that it cries on the outside and burns within?" Burning candles are described as crying. And the Yi Dynasty official Wang Bang-yŏn (王邦衍), in the line "Last night the crying stream shed tears," heard the sound of a brook flowing as loud crying. Admiral Yi Sun-sin, who has been called the greatest Korean naval hero, in his "Diary in Wartime" shed tears, saying, "Crying, crying, waiting only for death." As in the Silla song "Epitaph Dedicated to Chukji" (慕竹旨郎歌), "Everything weeps longing for the past spring." There are tears in every tree and grass, in the endless reverberations of a bell, and in the sound of a stream. Perhaps we have heard everything in this way because we are a people of many sorrows.

There is a proverb "The hand spinning-wheel eats up the cotton while its sounds are like crying." How many tears have welled up in the hearts of spinning girls as they turned wheels under the dim lamp? So the girls heard the sound of the click-clack of the spinning wheel as the sound of sobbing, and saw their own fate in the features of the wheel as it devoured the cotton. Thus what they must do helplessly in tears is termed "crying while eating up cotton."

A certain scholar of Korean literature indicated that "The custom of our people is that everything begins and ends with crying." When a person dies, he continues, "the first and the fifteenth days of the month are traditionally set aside as days of crying" and "one should mourn from the day of death until the coffin leaves the house. The day after the burial one mourns under the pretext that it is the beginning of the mourning period, and on the third day one also mourns. Afterwards on each first and fifteenth of the month one must offer sacrifices to one's ancestors with crying." They don't mourn simply, but according to a very "musical manner," a formalized ritual of weeping. Even when it is not a memorial day, when we hear the rural women complain and sob, we marvel afresh at their wonderfully delicate compositions with varied tempos, like the *Yukjabaegi* folksongs and the *sinawi* rhythms. A son is dutiful when he cries, as is a loyal subject and a faithful widow. Perhaps this has given rise to the hypothesis that "if you don't cry, you are not Korean."

In my country, where there were no dance parties, even love was expressed with tears. Most of the old love stories begin in this fashion: "One dim moonlit night a frail woman sobs in an isolated house. A stranger hears the sound of this crying and asks the woman why she is so sad...." In this way love begins to blossom with a

6

lonely widow. Are tears a harmonizing pill which will solve the relations between the sexes? As in the proverb "Tears fill the vale," so tears cover our land.

This is evident in the most trifling movie or in radio soap operas where no other country can equal our crying part. The crying action is such that any actor can do it wonderfully. This is because what we have inherited from our ancestors is this ability for crying and tears.

Why on earth do we have to cry this way? And why do we glamorize our crying and bring our tears into our daily lives, and how in these tears did we forge our morals? Can we say that our arts and culture sprouted forth and grew in the tears clear as crystal?

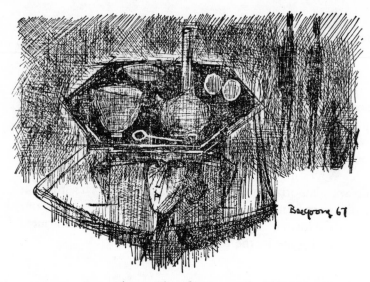

Baegom 67

3. In the Shadow of Hunger

OUR sorrow and tears in large measure came from poverty and hunger. Poverty and hunger play a role of great importance in popular proverbs which have been handed down from mouth to mouth. Like the proverb, we have thought "Whatever anyone says, there is no greater sorrow than hunger."

Watch the Korean children. Their stomachs are disproportionately large in comparison with their arms and legs—naked and bloated stomachs distended like a drum, with the watermelon seeds they have eaten still stuck on them; this is the symbol of our sorrow.

The Korean children with their bloated stomachs do not seem to indulge in childish fantasies even when they watch birds flying in the blue sky. What comes from their lips are not songs of angels but a bitter lament on hunger.

> *O Stork, O Stork, what do you eat?*
> *We borrow rice from our neighbors.*
> *When will you pay it back?*
> *I'll buy it in the market and pay it back later.*

They grew up with this kind of song. All problems lie in "eating." Wherever we went the dark shadow of hunger followed us.

It's just the same today. Kindergarten children sing with lovely voices. Although they don't know worldly stains and pain, still their songs express worry and concern about hunger.

> *Rabbit, Rabbit in the mountain.*
> *What do you eat in winter?*

Many of our folksongs about animals are also related to eating.

> *O Pheasant, Pheasant, Mr. Pheasant*
> *With your sons and daughters*
> *What do you eat?*
> *Beans from the front fields,*
> *I eat and live like this.*

> *Let's eat rice cake, Owl*
> *There is no grain, whooo*
> *Don't worry, whooo*
> *I'll borrow it, whooo.*
> *When will you pay it back?*
> *I'll pay it back in autumn, whooo.*

Even when they are full of dreams, Korean children

unconsciously have to sing about eating. When one's birthday comes around, be it in a wealthy or a poor family, it has become a ceremony to give rice piled high in bowls. It must have been a tearful present that one should eat to the full at least on one's birthday.

Another saying has it that "The back of the head of the departing guest is beautiful." Wasn't such an expression created because there was not enough food? All adults' and children's interest therefore had to be concentrated naturally on food.

It is funny that we call our families "eating mouths" (食口). The English word "family" comes from the word for "servant," while ours comes from "mouths which eat rice." With the word for "family" we just count the mouths we have to feed.

Our language of tastes, reflecting these circumstances, demonstrates a unique development. No matter how rich a country is in vocabulary, the people may not be fortunate enough to distinguish such differences as "bitter" (쓰다), " sourly bitter" (씁슬하다), "terribly bitter" (쓰디쓰다), and "sweet" (달다), "dully sweet" (들큰하다), "pleasantly sweet" (달콤하다) and "sweetish" (달짝지근하다).

We alone are able to express in words the distinctions of such complicated and delicate tastes. To begin with, how many ways do we use the term "to eat"? We age (eat age 나이먹다), are affected by the heat (eat heat 더위먹다), we embezzle (eat public money 公金먹다) and, worst of all, we are blamed (eat slander 辱먹다).

Even in the evaluation of people's character we use expressions derived from the taste of food. To wit: He is bland, somewhat silly and uninteresting (saltless guy 싱거운 놈); he is excessively prudent and rigid (salty or caustic guy 짠 놈); or, he is stern and strict (a hot, peppery guy 매운 놈). Foreigners, upon learning this, are sure to take us for cannibals.

In fine, our grief comes from the physical rather than the spiritual. Or if we were to use more technical terminology, it is not a metaphysical sorrow but a physical "cry." That sorrow comes more often than joy is illustrated in the proverb "The fingernails grow whenever there is sorrow, and the toenails grow when there is joy." This metaphor came from the way fingernails grow faster than toenails. If we analyze it in depth, we know that joy and sorrow are not mental growth, but what control physical growth.

The English word "sad" comes from the German *satt*. The etymology of that word is the same as "satiate." While our sorrow is the same, how different it is in dimension! Our sadness stems from hunger, but theirs is a sadness of a mental or metaphysical sort from repletion or boredom.

Homer's *Odyssey* has such a scene. Odysseus, after monster Scylla has devoured six soldiers, barely escapes and beaches his ship on Helios Island. Odysseus' party, suffering from hunger, prepares food and eats it. It is only after their stomachs are full that they begin to think of their dead friends and cry.

Although the origin of the word "sadness" in the West comes from being satiated, our crying comes before we are filled and our belts are tightened.

So our tears are neither romantic nor poetic; they

are prosaic, so very prosaic, and so often there is crying in real life. Isn't the word "tear" itself prosaic? It means water flowing from the eyes (eye-water 눈물). For a running nose we say "snot" (nose-water 콧물), an insipid and prosaic word.

The English "tear" and the French *larme* are independent words, while only "tear" in Korean strangely is a compound word composed of "eye" and "water" (눈＋물).

Although countless tears have flowed, our tears, which we have wiped on the bows of our stained clothes, cannot be the objects of beauty any more than the plain water flowing from the eyes. Even aesthetics is not permitted for tears shed on a hungry stomach. "See the Diamond Mountains on a full stomach,"[1] says the proverb.

---

1 Reputed to be the most beautiful scenery in Korea. Now in north Korea.

4. The Tragedy of Playing *Yut*

Translator's note: Yut is a game played by two or more players or teams of players with four sticks which are thrown in the air together and which, by falling face up or down, collectively determine how many spaces a player may move on the board towards a goal called "home." A player who lands on the same space as his opponent is said to "eat" his opponent and forces him to begin all over again. Landing on the same space as a member of your own team gives one the advantage of moving the two pieces at the same time with one throw of the sticks. *Yut* is a game much played in Korea —from wealthy homes, where the sticks may be of ivory, to the village, where they can be made from the rudest materials. It is played any time, but especially on holidays and most often on the New

Year. It is said that it originally had a fortune-telling or divination function in very early days.

WE like to play *yut*. It has been a custom since the period of the Three Kingdoms. But there seems to be a very Korean tragedy in the game. Each time we cast the *yut* sticks, they fall sometimes up and sometimes down, thus drawing a chart of fortune. Once the sticks are cast, they never can be changed or redone. If number one comes up, then it is simply number one; and if it is number two, that's it. Sometimes the *yut* game changes a divination of our fortune. Western dice are just the same in that aspect; that is, the fateful number is cast against chance. The origin of the word "dice" seems to contain the meaning "given by fate." All the same, we can say that *yut* is a degree more complicated than dice even if both are determined by chance.

Although each of the six faces of the die indicates an independent fate, the *yut* sticks combine with each other and that intricate relationship forms a definite meaning. Each *yut* stick, when cast, lands either face up or face down, indicating one's luck, and this combination may be called a unified and total fate. Although dice stand alone, the *yut* sticks can be said to have a unified destiny.

The nature of this interlocked destiny is a symbol of Korea, especially of the Korean social environment. While the strength which permeates the West lies in individual heroism, in the East, especially in Korea, power and fortune in life are determined by the dictates of the interlocked fate of the group rather than the individual.

14

If we sit and watch the *yut* sticks fall, they open before our eyes the four-party factional struggles of the Yi Dynasty. Individual luck will take one nowhere. If the fate of one's political party was good, be it the Eastern, Western, Southern or Northern, one might get power; but if one's fortune was bad, the party members traveled the same road of bitter destruction together.

Take the case of Yi Sun-sin[1], who joined the armed forces, but as a victorious admiral could not return home because his party was out of power. His fate was determined by the withered Southern faction.

This national tragedy is more vividly hinted at when we see the pieces move on the board than when we see the fateful *yut* sticks fall and roll to a stop. This is because we can say that the *yut* board is the epitome of the sanguinary factional struggles.

In *yut*, which is different from dice, the game is in the elimination of the leading pieces from the board. We play this game perhaps because of the fun of eliminating the enemy's pieces.

When the leading piece is taken by the scruff of the neck, as it were, and eliminated just before it is about to reach the goal in this bloody trial, one side bursts out in applause, while the other side moans out mortified laments.

The reality of the *yut* board is that the leading piece

---

1. Admiral Yi (1545–1598) invented the turtle boat and defeated the Japanese fleet in 1592. He is the most popular military hero of Korean history. Jailed for being a member of the Southern faction, he was recalled from jail to fight the Japanese. Even after he was victorious he was treated as a prisoner because of political factionalism.

always has a handicap, whence ensues uneasiness. Thus the guy who catches his opponent is next to get caught and, if one catches a piece, it all starts over again.

In this procedure of catching and being caught, the winner is the one who runs away quickly from the fateful *yut* board to the goal, much like in political strife. Is this all?

In the bloody struggle we act relentlessly, resorting to dirty tricks; but to our partners we display the tender principle of carrying them along by moving two pieces at once and being carried by them. This carrying along of one piece by another is *yut's* most lucky and pleasurable moment. This dual movement with our side and ganging-up on our opponents on the *yut* board—chase or being chased—reminds us of such Yi Dynasty politicians as Yu Cha-kwang, Kim Chong-jik's group, Cho Kwang-cho who died spitting blood, and Chŏng Ch'ŏl.[2]

The reality of political struggle, like the game of *yut*, is just one more thing that moves us to tears. The common people went hungry and cried out, while the wealthy ones and the intelligentsia, caught in the black whirlpool of political struggle in which whole clans were annihilated, also cried out. The breath of life at that time meant nothing more than literally "breathing in the throat." In a society where the symbol of reality was just like the proverb on playing *yut*—"Don't split a gut when

2. Yu Cha-kwang (?–1512), a villainous retainer who was later exiled. Kim Chong-jik(1431–1492), a famous scholar and politician in King Sŏngchong's regime. Cho Kwang-cho (1482–1519) was exiled by another faction's intrigue and was put to death by the king. Chŏng Ch'ŏl (Chŏng Song-kang, 1536–1593) had been exiled several times because of factional struggle.

16

you almost win because the game's not over yet"—there cannot be an everlastingly happy victor. As a result, the hungry commoners went to the mountains to gather roots and bark to eat and the literati went to the mountains to flee from political strife. Thus the country turned into a lonely landscape inhabited by beggars and hermits seeking "floating clouds and wild cranes," the beauty of nature.

This is perhaps why we use the expression "it is passable" (괜찮다) instead of "it is good" (좋다). The former is a shortened version of the statement "I do not want to be involved."

If one were involved with reality or in national affairs, one lost one's life. Even innocent wives and children were punished for undeserved crimes, and one had to live in exile with only the *kŏmunko*[3] to comfort his tears. It was therefore best not to become involved. One did not sing hymns to the wind and the moon because one loved nature, but because one could not survive otherwise. Like the sorrow of hunger, while in reality following our destiny, in the game we desperately take off the board those pieces which go ahead of us—truly the tragedy of *yut* is close upon us.

---

3. The *kŏmunko* is a long zither with six strings played with a type of bow. Its invention is credited to the Korean musician Wang San-ak of the Koguryŏ period. The earliest *kŏmunko* representation is found in a mural painting in a pre-7th century Koguryŏ tomb.

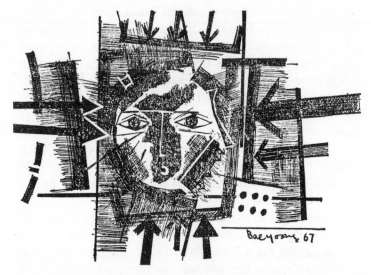

Baeyoong 67

5. The Shrimp in the Eastern Sea

IT'S strange. Unlike other people, we have been especially conscious of the geographical shape of our country. The shape of the peninsula, which is often compared to a rabbit[1], is used in the design of newspaper mastheads and even as the trademark on rubber shoes and everywhere else. On the wall of the bedroom of a dilapidated thatched hut we sometimes find the shape of the Korean peninsula embroidered with rose-of-sharon flowers and leaf designs. Although the embroidery is clumsy and the flyspecked frame so very poor, it somehow contains the desires of the people and touches our hearts.

1. The map of Korea looks like a rabbit facing west with its large ears to the north. It is a common symbol of Korea.

Of course, the French have loved the Seine, and the Germans have made a myth of the Rhine. But these are only a part of their territory. To carve the country's shape like an emblem or to praise it as "Three thousand *li* of magnificent landscape"[2] is rare indeed.

Even in the Japan of the past when chauvinism ran wild, they used as emblems their wooden clogs, the *geta*, or the peak of Mount Fuji or the cherry blossoms; but the geographical configuration of the country was not emphasized.

Actually there is a sad reason why we have behaved thus: granted that the geographical shape is beautiful and unique, it is chiefly because we have worried keenly about the possible disappearance of our land.

China is a vast land fifty times larger than ours; there are also the wide plains of the north where powerful nomadic tribesmen rose and fell—how could we not be concerned about the fate of our country, a people living on a small peninsula stretching out from a corner of Asia?

Obsession with aggression has continued from the beginning of our history. We do not mention 3000 *li* because our country is so big or so small. This is neither pride nor a lament; it is assurance and a kind of reaffirmation.

When our land was taken by the Japanese, and now that our country is divided, the shape of the rabbit which is carved in our hearts and the image of this clump of earth called "three thousand *li*" is indelible.

When we hear the children loudly singing the anthem

2. A *li* is approximately one-third of a mile. "Three thousand *li*" is a common expression used in describing Korea.

"The peninsula of three thousand *li*," it is like an appeal to the people of the world that "This land is ours, please keep your hands off it."

When we open the map of Asia and study it, it reminds us why we have lived all our lives in suffering. Our geographical position is a fateful one. We know that this has given rise to the proverb "When whales fight, the shrimp suffers."

As we may know from the position of the Great Wall of China, which divided the Asian continent into north and south, wars waged continuously. In the north were the empires of the wild nomadic tribes, the Mongols and the Hsiungnu; in the south was the great agricultural empire, China. They fought for power continuously. Unfortunately, since this peninsula was placed on the eastern border of the north-south powers, it had to be in the position of a sad shrimp.

That is the way it is. Our nation was not a "rabbit," but a "shrimp." If the shrimp wants to survive, she must quickly weigh the two powers and attach herself to the stronger one. People castigate this approach as "toadyism," but without it the lonely shrimp in the Eastern Sea would have had no future for a single moment.

The Koryŏ Dynasty survived by attaching itself to the Chinese Sung Dynasty in the south, and when the Liao in the north became strong, it had to ally with them. When the Yüan became powerful, Koryŏ then had to change again.

The fate of this country which had to serve the master of the continent, whether we liked it or not, swung back and forth time after time like a pendulum to the master nation—from the Yüan to the Ming, and from the Ming to the Ch'ing in the north-south power groupings.[3]

Although we had our own nation, we couldn't even use the reign titles for our own kings.

While living by *nunch'i*,[4] we still had to suffer from aggression and oppression compounded, and each time the bud of our culture was nipped. In recent centuries our relations, caught between Japan and Russia, have become more complicated.

We have a country, but we are really a wandering group. Now there are no north and south groups; instead the shrimp is caught in the eastern and western whales' struggles. Our people have not been able to say "We are masters of this land." The "wanderers in their own fatherland" can only affirm that this is their land by uttering "three thousand *li*" or by looking at the shape of the country drawn in newspapers or on the bottom of rubber shoes.

These have been the tears of our people, sobbing from hunger... the tears of political struggle like playing *yut*, and crying from not being able to call our fatherland "my fatherland." Our tears were shed in all our earth and in all our wind.

Author's note: A Japanese historian named Mikami Tsukio,

---

3. The Koryŏ (918–1392) was a Korean kingdom, while the others mentioned were Chinese or became sinicised empires; the Liao (907–1168), the Sung (960–1278), the Yüan (1280–1368), Ming (1368–1644) and Ch'ing (1644–1911).
4 See Chapter 7.

noting Korea's unfortunate geographical position, once wrote about Japan's benefit from the Korean peninsula:

"When we open a geography of Asia and the areas bordering the Pacific, the Korean peninsula is like the breast of the mother continent, Asia. A drop of milk from that breast became Tsushima and another Iki Island. If we look at it in this way, the Japanese islands are like an infant in his mother's arms. Although Korea has had the benefit of letting north Asian and Chinese culture penetrate without barrier because Korea was connected with the continent, when there was a strong political power, then Korea had to become subject to it and when there was a unified kingdom in China, Korea became so unfortunate as to fall under this irresistable force."

In modern times we cannot forget that Korea has been damaged because she has been a bridge by which the Japanese pushed onto the mainland.

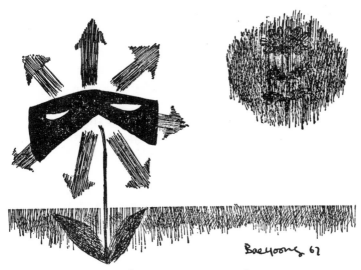

Baeyoong 67

6. On the Names of
Grasses and Flowers

ON a dark and quiet night a single flower blooms beside a stream or by a path. At times its paleness seems like moonlight and at other times, a subdued yellow. Why does it bloom only at night having ignored so many days? People have told romantic and sorrowful tales of this flower and have given it a beautiful name. They say it is the soul of a nymph who loved the moon.

She longed for the moon so much that she was jealous of the stars and finally Zeus became angry. He exiled her to a place where there was no moon and no stars. So the moon pined for the nymph and searched for her.

Zeus saw this and interfered with their love by sending clouds and rain. The nymph kept yearning and day by day got thinner until she finally died, and her soul was buried on a hill. There a single plant grew and a sad flower bloomed alone waiting for the moon in the dark of night. It is what is called "the moon greeting flower" (the evening primrose).

However, we Koreans have named this flower "the robber flower." Of course, these days we also call it "the moon greeting flower," but this is simply a translation from the Chinese.

The common people, who have had a life of bare subsistence, do not see in the flowers the appearance of a lover waiting for the moon, but the face of bitter reality. While other flowers all quietly slumber in the dark, this flower alone blooms. The people thought this suspicious, so they thought it must have been a "robber."

Flowers and grasses are the common people's myths. The weeds and those flowers which bloom freely by the roadside are more loved by people because they are not decorative or enticing. So, in some countries flowers and plants naturally evoke beautiful folk tales and beautiful names. In these are entangled earthy feelings and the people's poetry.

But the flowers and plants in our country are like the case of the "robber flower"— more than beautiful, the names are cheap, and more than poetic, many are prosaic. Why did they give a name like "robber" to a weak and slender plant? In the names such as "robber's hook" and "robber's stick" what we feel is not a warm glance but rather a sight full of brutality and precaution.

The names taken from the Chinese, like the Jade Hairpin Flower (Plaintain Lily) and the Phoenix Flower (Bal-

24

sam), are somewhat beautiful. But pure Korean names are like trash, such as "daughter-in-law's toilet paper" (*persicaria senticosa*), "daughter-in-law's belly button" (*polygonum perfoliatum*), "rat's urine" (*valeriana dagoletiana*), "chicken's toilet paper" (*commelina communis*) and "frog's toenail" (*semiaquilegia adoxoides*). Sometimes they weren't satisfied with that and, what is worse, there are many names such as "dog's testicles" and "bachelor's X" (*asparagus lucidus*). At most, a beautiful flower is compared to a *kisaeng* and described as a "*kisaeng* plant." We see a bright firefly like dew on a bush on a summer's night and usually call it a "dog's dung worm;" we blush about our poor imagination. The folk songs about plants and flowers are also the same as this.[1]

> *The "bong bong" breaking-wind mulberry*
> *The "sal sal" breaking-wind bush clover*
> *The anus mugwort*

> or

> *The bloody linden slashed-by-a-sword*
> *The stuck-in-the-throat thorn bush*
> *The trembling popular*
> *The dried-out bamboo*
> *The sat on and crushed boxthorn*
> *The kissing, smack, smack, indigo plant.*

When we saw plants, we thought of them as breaking

---

1. Bishop Rutt (*The Korea Times,* June 29, 1967) wrote "The cowslip and oxslip of England have names that mean dung... the *pissenlit* of France is familiar enough; and on a more sophisticated level the etymology of the name orchid may offer a shock to those unprepared."

wind or shedding blood, or as wrinkled or trembling, or as ghastly.

When we look at the beautiful yet homely pumpkin flower, we say "Pumpkin, pumpkin, your flower is bitter and my flower is sweet." And even of the azalea which symbolizes our emotion they sing:

> *Flower, flower, azalea flower*
> *You shun the plains*
> *Why do you bloom among the rocks?*
> *I hate the plains*
> *The rocks are closer to my nature.*

The exclusive and selfish song like "Your flower is bitter and mine is sweet" and the song of the azalea which likes to bloom among the narrow rocks more than the open plains, show escape to a hermit life. Within these songs there is cold heartedness which is cut off from the joy of positive life and generosity.

We have few names of beautiful plants and legends and folksongs, and this means that our myths, and thus our imagination, are poor.

This is because our common people, who have been chased by hunger and who have struggled against oppressive rulers, have not had enough leisure to create their own myths. People's happiness and their real life are not just a matter of eating and sleeping; beyond that is the pursuit of joy. It seems to us that the objective of the ideal life is just the ease of the animal existence of eating and sleeping. So, although it was an insult for people to spend repeated days in just eating and sleeping, it was happiness for our common people. So when we write a letter, we ask "Are you eating and sleeping the same as ever?"

In a life in which one is only busy with problems of eating and sleeping, there is no spare time to produce myths and legends. In all our aspects there is no free time and this, I think, is the key to solving the problem of our way of thinking and way of life.

Baeyoong 67

7. Living by *Nunch'i*

Translator's note: Nunch'i, literally eye-measure, is both
the feelings and the manners of a person and it is also,
in verb form, to study the attitudes and emotions
of another person so that you may know how to
respond. In the second sense, it is therefore something
like the sizing up of a situation, but it forms a
more central core of Korean thought.

W E are a people with a developed sense of *nunch'i;* as
the proverb says, "If you have a quick sense of *nunch'i,*
you can even eat pickled shrimp in a Buddhist temple."[1]
Our way of thinking is one in which we value *nunch'i*
more highly than logic or analytic power.

---

1. This type of food is prohibited inside the precincts of a
   Buddhist temple because it involves taking life.

Nunch' i is a kind of "sense," but it cannot simply be explained as "sense." *Nunch' i* is an indication of the weaker examining the feelings of the stronger, necessary in an unreasonable society in which logic, principles and rules have no place.

When a commoner is arrested and taken to an official's house, the best policy is to look at the official's *nunch' i*. It is meaningless to insist on our nation's fundamental logic and principles or argue whether or not there was a crime. That is rather cutting off your nose to spite your face. The important thing is to fathom what is in his mind with your own quicker *nunch' i*. You cannot ask openly.

This is true with punishment by flogging in the past. Suppose one is to receive ten strokes; but all depends on the feeling of the one who does the flogging. It is possible that one hundred strokes on the hip will produce no swelling, while ten strokes may undo one. One's fate is completely at the mercy of *nunch' i*.

Also, we must have *nunch' i* in giving a bribe. If *nunch' i* is lacking, one will go bankrupt by offering one hundred pieces of cash when only ten pieces should do. Or the same person faces even more serious disaster by offering ten pieces when one hundred is required.

High government officials also had to see the king's *nunch' i*. When they attended office, more than anything else they had to watch secretly the expression on the royal face through the folds of their robes as they bowed their heads. They had to be careful and avoid outspoken admonition when the king was in a bad mood. When they saw that the king was pleased, they could not fail to take

29

the opportunity to submit a difficult petition. When the *nunch'i* clearly did not fit the situation, then one could lose one's head or suffer the extermination of one's family.

Our king also had to look at the *nunch'i* of the suzerain power. With a dour *nunch'i* the fate of the nation would be in peril. Without *nunch'i*, from the commoner to the king, one could not live for even one day.

Thus, intuition developed more than logic, and the sensitivity of grasping all these signs developed more than reason. Like the point of a needle, the keenness of the sense of observing another's *nunch'i* is the point.

For example, just before the Japanese invasion of 1592, we only examined by *nunch'i* whether or not Japan would commit aggression. Our ambassadors, sent to Japan to spy the situation, even after half a year's stay only saw Hideyoshi's eyes. They just examined his *nunch'i*. In their report to the throne on which the life and death of the country depended, the envoy Hwang Yun-gil (黃允吉) said, "Seeing the flashes in his eyes, it seems that Hideyoshi is bound to invade our country" while Kim Sŏng-il (金誠一)[2] said, "He is not the kind of person who is able to invade because his eyes are like those of a rat."

When the Japanese ambassadors came, they carefully spied on the lack of national discipline by comparing the length of the Korean troops' spears with that of the Japanese, the way in which Korean officials played with *kisaeng* girls and the stupid manner in which public

---

2. Hwang Yun-gil (1536– ?) was a well-known scholar in the Sŏncho Period, and Kim Sŏng-il (1538–1593) was a politician at that time.

officials competed with one another to get black pepper[3] thrown at official receptions by the Japanese—while our ambassadors only looked at Hideyoshi's eyes and quarreled over the possibility of his invasion. The method of thinking of the Japanese who observed Korea was analytical and scientific, while that of our ambassadors was intuitive and impressionistic. They didn't analyze Japanese government policy or their natural resources, but instead hinted at the Japanese way of thinking by phrenological interpretation; would Korea be invaded or were Hideyoshi's eyes like those of a tiger or a rat?

This is not all. When Korea received a letter from Hideyoshi which said, "We cannot live for more than one hundred years. How can we live couped up on this island? We will spread our customs throughout the four hundred districts of China waving our swords over the Ming," the court quarreled whether or not to report it to the Ming. It was a war between two parties, whether to fathom Ming or Japan. No one thought of how to check and avoid Hideyoshi's ambition to invade the mainland, or what the fate of Korea would be when war broke out. Instead they were concerned with Ming China's feelings—if Ming felt badly, what would happen to us. The core of the problem lay in the observation of someone else's *nunch'i*. We could have escaped the ghastly disasters of the war if we had handled it by relying upon scientific judgment, not on *nunch'i*. We could have allowed the Ming to station their troops in Korea or quietly let them pass through Korea, thus profiting from the situation.

3. Black pepper was an item of extreme rarity and therefore very precious.

Even today we still have the *nunch'i* way-of-thinking. In the office we still look at the *nunch'i* of the president of the firm, the people do the same with officials, and the officials to the higher officials and the government looks at America's *nunch'i*. Many still live according to the proverb, "If you have a quick sense of *nunch'i*, you can even eat pickled shrimp in a temple."

Author's note: French everyday life is conducted by what they call "good sense" (*bon sense*), and the English depend upon "common sense." But *nunch'i* is very different from either of these two. *Nunch'i* has no relation to logic. *Nunch'i* goes one step beyond good sense or common sense. It does not depend on your own standard of common sense and intelligence, but whether my attitude and manner are acceptable to the other person. Foreigners do not compromise or concede when it is contrary to their common sense, regardless of the rank of the other person. But in our case if we try to explain something to a superior with common sense, this is regarded as impertinent and accusatory.

Therefore, there was no other way but to solve problems with *nunch'i*.

8. "Save A Man" and "Help Me"

WHEN a person is drowning or unexpectedly meets with some disaster, he unconsciously calls out for help. Although it is more of a shriek than words, it is still quite different from that of an animal. Because it is a human cry, however short it may be, there must be a hidden meaning, and this meaning differs from country to country.

Englishmen say "help me," Japanese say "give help" (*Tasukete Kure*), Koreans say "save a man" (*Saram Sallyŏ* 사람 살려). When we study these short expressions, we are able to know a great deal about the national way of

33

thought of each country. "Help me" and "give help" both mean requests for help; the only difference is that in English it means "give *me* help," while in Japanese it is simply "to ask for *help*." It seems evident that the individual consciousness of the Westerner who wants support for himself when wandering at the brink of death is more intense than that of the Japanese who is an Asian, although the meaning of "give help" is not different.

Unlike the Korean expression "save a life," the expressions "help me" and "give help" obviously ask for added strength. The meaning latent in "help me" and "give help" is asking for assistance due to a lack of strength, not for relief starting from zero. It is an attitude which doesn't lose a sense of identity even at the edge of death. Although "asking for help" and "save a life" are the same, how different they are in meaning and attitude! When we meet with an emergency, we only plead to be saved. It is an attitude of complete despair, powerlessness and self surrender.

If we put it another way, the expression "save a man" means "I don't have any strength" and "I am dying." The request for being saved, not the request for help, is an expectation of 100% relief. Unlike giving fertilizer to a tree or a stick to an old man, it is rather like carrying on the back a person who has fallen down and is almost dead. It is an act of absolutely entrusting one's body, one's life and one's fate to another. It is tantamount to receiving relief from others, supposing oneself to be dead. We have heard the "save a man" type of cry too often and we still hear it. An example is the proverb "If you starve for three days, someone will come with food on his back." If we only sit and go hungry, someday a man will come carrying food for us. The man who comes literally will not come to help the starving person, but to save him.

This has applied to our country as a whole. Whenever we had a war, we asked for troops from other countries. But this was not a "request for assistance," but a "request to be saved." Were those troops coming to assist us as allies? No. If we look at the history of the Japanese invasion of 1592, we shed bloody tears not only because of Japanese tyranny, but because of the violent aggression of the troops of the Chinese Ming Dynasty which came to help us. How did our King feel when he went to Uisun-gwan to meet the Ming General Li Jusung? How about the dignity of our great and noble King when he said to the general, "The fate of our country is in your hands; please defend us from the enemy?" How about our dignity too when the generals spat out complaints that the King himself did not greet each of the forty Ming generals? When our people had nothing to eat, the Ming troops, using the weather as an excuse, indulged in depraved orgies rather than fighting the war. But what complaint have we, who "asked to be saved," to make against the Chinese reinforcements?

Today America compares assistance to Korea to "pouring water into a bottomless jar." Both sides think of this not as economic assistance but as "an act of feeding and keeping us alive." Nothing differs between today and a hundred years ago. As Toynbee said, the verb "awake" is both intransitive and transitive. Neither outside strength alone nor self-strength alone will help us open our eyes; assistance precisely corresponds to this "awakening process." However much you stimulate a dead body, its eyes cannot be opened. Only when a person is conscious of opening his eyes will his eyes finally be opened. When "to awaken someone" and "to open one's own eyes" are combined, assistance from one's neighbors becomes real assistance. "Asking for help" should not cause shame. The problem is that our concept of assistance, which has lost its sense of self-identity, has controlled us.

Author's note: Korean parents try to help and interfere with their children's private lives. But in the United States even if the father is a millionnaire, it is a common-place that the son has to wash dishes to earn his tuition.

Also in America children are very much left to themselves and so they learn self-responsibility and self-reliance. Even when they ride in an automobile, parents sit in front and the children are in back; but in the case of Korea, usually children sit between the parents.

9. Legends of "Momotaro" and "The Sun and Moon"

THE lonely children of this colony during the Japanese occupation grew up hearing two different legends. In school they studied the Japanese stories of "Momotaro" and "Issunboshi"(lit. the "One inch tall hero"), and when they returned home, by the dim candle light, they heard Korean stories of the brother and sister who were chased by a tiger. The stories in Japanese always had elements of aggression and scheming, while ours were filled with sadness and disaster.

Momotaro, the child born from a peach, with a sword and rice cakes alone conquers a ghost castle. Issunboshi, only a dwarf not more than one inch tall, encounters a strong goblin using a needle as a sword and a teacup as a boat. The Japanese stories always end with the triumphant return of a hero in a golden carriage or with a marvelous treasure stick.

We were envious of such stories. How was it possible for a little child to defeat a strong ghost? And so much gold... Momotaro's rice cake and sword are symbols of Japanese trickery and militarism, and the defeat of a nine-foot goblin by the dwarf hints at the aggressive nature of the island country intending to belittle and advance into the Asian mainland. Japan, alone and barehanded, attacked Korea, China and even the world. How dare they, they who are so small... not even one inch tall!

It was not in the schoolroom where the Japanese flag was hung, but in the poor room covered with bloody spots caused by bedbugs that the Korean children heard the stories of the sun and the moon, stories in which a mother was first stripped of her red bean cake by a tiger as she went over a hill, and then her arms, legs and finally her life. The tiger, dressed in the mother's clothes, tried to eat up the children who were waiting for their mother.

The children who heard this story cried. Annoyed at the mother who was always deceived, they sympathized with the children who were chased while they resented the violent tiger. The helpless brother and sister tried to escape by climbing a tree, but there again they were not safe. There was no escape. The children prayed to god, "God, god, if you want to save us, send us a new rope, hung from heaven so we can climb up; but if you want us to die, send us a rotten rope so we fall to earth "

There was nothing they could do with their own strength, and God sent a new rope, "so the brother and sister ascended into the sky and she became the moon and he became the sun."

The story finally ends in their ascension into the sky after being chased over the earth. It is a story not of aggression but of suffering, and not of restoration on earth but escape into the heavens. It is the story of our people who, through the aggression of the Japanese such as Momotaro and Issunboshi, lost their mother and home and finally had to flee to a foreign land.

The story of "The Sun and Moon" is only one of such stories. The suffering of the naive saltseller cheated by the fox, and that of the girl Arang, executed wrongly by an official, who appears before a governor as a ghost with dishevelled hair—are similar tales.

This is also true if we compare the national anthems of the two countries. The Japanese sing "Until a pebble becomes a rock..." while we sing "Until the Eastern Sea runs dry and Mount Paekdu wears away..." Although both are concerned with eternity, theirs is an eternity described as growth, while ours is one of decay. The Japanese thought of the future as aggression and prosperity, while we thought of it as suffering and destruction. The emotions of the two are very different.

Whether things are good or bad, we always end our expressions with "I'll die." If something is good, we say "It's so good I'll die"; if it is funny, "It's so funny I could die." When we are sad or exhausted, we, of course, use the same expression.

We have lived thinking of death, the extreme suffering. We were the people stripped of life and wealth by the sword and the rice cake of Momotaro—the Japanese.

Being a passive and good people, our last wish was not to lose hope in the midst of hardships. The Japanese don't say "I'll die," but use the expression *daijobu* or "It's OK." Although in speech it means "don't worry," the meaning of the Chinese characters is "a masculine man"(大丈夫). The Japanese say, "We are men; such things are not a problem to us who have a martial heart."

As Momotaro with a sweet rice cake ball lured the dog and the monkey and the pheasant, Issunboshi, on the one hand with an intimate smile and on the other with the cruelty of a sharp sword, waved a golden club.

As we trusted a rope descended from the sky, we have sadly sung the song, "Even though the string of beads breaks against a rock the string will never be severed." Our lives, emotions and feelings will continue like the string no matter what the hardships.

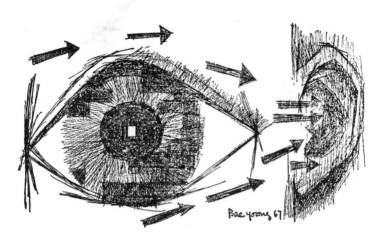

Bae yoons 67

10. A Culture of the Ear
and a Culture of the Eye

IN Korea, the most developed aspect of our language is
that of onomatopoetic words. This means our words are in
large part more aural than visual. We call the sky "blue"
but we also call the grass "blue." We don't often distinguish between blue and green.

But we do distinguish the aural aspects of Korean
with a delicacy of degree difficult to find in foreign languages. For example, when a number of people lie sleeping in the same room, we try to think of different words
to describe their breathing. A suckling babe breathes *saek-
saek*, a kindergarten schoolchild *k'olk'ol* and a father and
mother *k'ulk'ul*. Westerners who boast about their discovery of the atomic microscope actually can't subdivide

the sound of breathing as we can. They indicate the sound of young children or adults sleeping with only a "ZZZ."

Bells are just the same. Westerners at most say "*ding-dong,*" but we have onomatopoetic sounds through a whole range of vowels and consonants for this purpose. We even express the bell's reverberations with the onomatopoetic sounds *ttaengkŭrŏng ttaengkŭrŏng.*

Western languages are developed in logical aspects, while it has often been indicated that our language is developed in terms of emotion. When we give names to things, we often use an aural image.

Of course, even though in Western languages there are names of birds, like the cuckoo, which are given for the sound of their song, the examples are not as many as in Korean.[1] The cicada was called the *maemi* as it made the sound "*maemmaem;*" the frog was given the name *kaekuri* as it says "*kaekulkaekul;*" the woodpecker is *ttakttakuri,* the owl *puŏngi,* the cuckoo *ppŏkkuki,* the Siberian ruddy crane *ttŭmpuki,* the bushwarbler *kkoekkori,* the cricket *tsŭrŭrami....* We cannot even give the long list of such names, there are so many.

The gong itself is named after the sound *ching.* When we see the (Chinese) word for "light rain" (細雨), we think of it aurally and distinguish between a light drizzle, *posŭlpi* (보슬비), and a slightly heavier drizzle, *pusŭlpi* (부슬비). And even in this modern age we call a jet plane a *ssaekssaeki.* Although in writing we name the steamboat

---

1. See also H.B. Hulbert: "The whole range of onomatopoetic words, in which Korean is particularly rich, has never been reduced to Chinese..." "Korean Survivals," *Transactions of the Korea Branch of the Royal Asiatic Society,* 1900, vol. 1.

and the motorboat in accordance with their activities, we call them the *t'ongt'ongpae* and the *ttokttakpae*.

In English, when they want to say "I know," they say "I see"; they are people who live mainly by sight. But we say "obey!" (lit. hear my words well), "he doesn't obey" (lit. he doesn't hear my words well) and "he didn't understand" (lit. the ear is dark). It seems that we understand things by hearing and not by seeing. We also say of a machine which does or doesn't work well that it has no ears (lit. it hears well or it doesn't hear).

If this is so, then what in the world is the real difference between seeing and hearing?

Professor Pak Chong-hong of Seoul National University indicated in his thesis "On Seeing and Hearing" that seeing is *logos* and hearing is *pathos*. Thus, so to speak, a culture of the eye is intellectual, rational, theoretical and active, while a culture of the ear is emotional, sensitive, intuitive and passive.

The American poet Archibald MacLeish, in his radio drama *The Fall of the Cities*, said, "The eye is a realist. The eye cannot help connecting the preceding thing with the following thing. . . . The ear is a poet. The ear believes. It creates. And it believes."

If we ourselves believe this, then we can say that the culture of the eye is scientific and the culture of the ear is that of the poet.

Actually, this seems to be true. In Korea they say that there is no logic. They say that mathematics, which means science, does not exist. Instead there is emotion, intuitional insight and a soulful spirit. In the depths of hardship and loneliness Koreans have heard the sound of eternity. They accepted things as they were without measured calculating or analyzing. So, as in Professor Soetsu Yanagi's theory on the arts of a visual nature, isn't it true that our line, like the rhythm of the *kŏmunko*, is developed more than color and form?

Moreover, we are a people who are exceptionally fond of music. We see this when we read some of the old stories—like that of the robber who liked to play the flute, and the tiger who was trying to devour him but who was so entranced by the music of the flute that the robber's life was spared.

Our actions are not based upon coldly logical theory; we can say that our strength is rooted in warm emotional feeling.

The eye sees only what it wants to see. If it sees not or if it does not wish to see, that is the end of the matter. But the ear naturally hears all. Though this passivity is sometimes the seed of tragedy, on the other hand it has given us the refined wisdom of a purified spirit and a depth of emotion.

Bae yoons 67

11. The Meaning of Stone Walls

TAGORE thought that the culture of Western Europe
was a culture of walls; and he said that the culture of
ancient Greece was built up in city walls and that present
culture also began in a cradle of lime and bricks. He
also lamented that walls provide a sense of control and
also isolation between men. Because of the culture of walls,
countries are divided from other countries, knowledge from
knowledge, and people from nature. Because of this kind
of wall, people always wonder what is on the other side
and they will always fight violently to find out.

But he said that Indian civilization is different from
this, that it is not a culture of walls but a culture of the
forest. This culture is surrounded by vast, natural life. It
is one clothed in nature and in contact continuously and

45

intimately with various aspects of nature. So there is no iso-lation or division, no control and struggle; rather, it dwells as music, harmonious, saturating, inclusive and vast. The people of the forest culture are at one with the universe. They are not set in opposition to the earth or water, or to the sunlight, or to the fruit and flowers. They realize peace and empathy in harmony and unity. It is, so to speak, a culture of completeness.

When we hear Tagore's words, we think of our own stone walls. When Europeans from the "walled culture" first set foot on our earth, they were amazed by our rural stone walls. However poor or abject the thatched hut, there was always a wall around it. If there wasn't a stone wall, then there was an earth wall, and if there wasn't an earth wall, there was a woven reed wall screening the hut.

As everyone knows, our country is famous through-out the world for being mountainous. If we think of our fields, they are actually nothing more than borders con-necting one mountain with another, and if we think of our wide rivers and streams, they are nothing but valleys con-necting the mountains with the sea. Wherever we go, our pervasive mountains divide us like walls. Why did we learn the custom of building more walls on our narrow land?

Almost anywhere we can discover the remains of walls in any rural area. Ours is a situation in which our towns have stone wall fortifications, and our houses have stone walls, and again these walls in wealthy homes are further divided into walls with twelve gates.

But let's look for a moment at our walls. They never, as Tagore indicated, seem to be screens for solitude and division or for battle and control.

46

These stone walls of our country are neither high nor strong compared with those of Shanghai, which Lin Yu-t'ang called the third "Great Wall of Infinite Length." China's walls are higher than houses. However much you may, stand on tiptoe, you cannot see inside. They are completely secluded and fortified, which means a blockage against the outside. All Chinese have their walls and live within them.

On the other hand, our stone walls are higher and bigger than those of the Japanese. Around the Japanese thatched house there is in many cases no wall, and even if there is a wall, it is of reeds through which the inside can be seen clearly; there is no difference between this and an open house. As in the case of Europe, except for castles, walls are not stressed at all in private Japanese houses.

Our stone walls are in a median position between the closed and open ones. If you look in from outside you can half see the interior. Over the earth wall you may see the cockscomb and sunflowers and the upper part of the body of a girl coming out of the open door. The walls of our country may be said to be in the nature of a symbol for the "half-open" type where the interior scenery is sometimes seen and sometimes unseen. And how beautiful that scene is; a landscape of red dragonflies sitting on the brushwood gate and the green vines half veiling the white gourds hanging down over the stone wall. How decorative is this scene!

Do our walls serve to protect us from thieves? No, a thief can jump over this kind of wall. As Yi Sang, the novelist, pointed out, a burglar would lose his sense of burgling to rob such a poor house with such a stone wall.

47

Moreover, does the wall protect us against animals? No, in one corner of the wall there is usually some ordinary hole so a weasel or a stray cat can come and go freely. The wall simply is nothing but a boundary line. The wall does not divide and juxtapose "you" from "me" but is a means of alleviating emotional insecurity by drawing a boundary. Walls exist but they never give an image of isolation and resentment against others. This half-open nature of stone walls means unity in division, union in isolation, and openness in a closed state. In the boundary line of this hazy stone wall, so to speak, Korean culture has dimly grown—a stone wall culture, midway between the culture of fortified walls and the culture of the forest.

Bae Yoong Ly

12. *Kich'im* and Knocking

Translator's note: Kich'im (기침) is the natural act of
clearing one's throat and is used to call attention to
one's presence. It is usually given in English dialogue
by the expression "ahem" but may also be translated
as "coughing." While it is sometimes translated as
"coughing" here, it is also often kept in the original
Korean for clarity. It is a very polite method of
announcing oneself.

BASICALLY we Koreans do not knock. Knocking is a
custom of Westerners who respect the privacy of individual life. Although we have been used to this custom
for quite a long time, it has not been completely assimilated into our life, and sometimes we make mistakes. Too
often we open a bathroom door without knocking and we

49

meet with disgrace. When there is a knock from outside, we sometimes unconsciously answer "yes?" from the inside of the bathroom. Not only that, we have all met the "thunderer" who rushes in almost before we have heard the sound of his knock. All these are acts of complete nonsense.

On office doors there is often a sign saying "Knock efore entering"—perhaps because of the many rascals who enter without knocking. This is also farcical.

Although forcing someone to knock is laughable, it is just as strange to require knocking at an office which is not even a private room. What on earth is going on in an office that we should knock? Is some kind of a plot or counterfeiting taking place there? Is someone making love to a working girl? If it isn't this, are there nudists working there?

Asking someone to knock can be construed as announcing the existence of one's personal and private secrets. This is because the words "Knock before entering" correspond to pasting up a notice which says "Behind this door we are now perpetrating some scandalous act which others shouldn't see."

Actually, knocking itself is like an ostrich sticking his head in the sand. Let's suppose one knocks at the door of a girl who is living alone. If we take an extreme view, he is actually suspicious of that girl's behavior. Granted this is not the case, still he may be imagining the shape of the girl's body. The sound of knocking is asking "Aren't you perhaps naked now?" or "Aren't you perhaps kissing someone?"

And it is also a warning "Please be careful. I am coming in now." Furthermore, when a knock is heard, if there is no answer from inside and it is as quiet as a dead mouse, we can easily guess at what is taking place.

Although Westerners think of knocking as one kind of etiquette, when we try to analyze the psychology of knocking, I don't think it is an especially noble kind of etiquette. The act of knocking itself is already a loss of etiquette.

In our country we have used a more noble method of knocking. It is veritably the sound of *kich'im*. How subtly different it is from openly knocking! In the old days, people without exception would give a loud but gentle "ahem" when they would enter a living room or a bathroom. There is no question but that there is no difference between the two as a signal warning others to be careful that someone is entering. But unlike knocking, which is a direct approach, *kich'im* remains at all times a quiet and warm suggestion.

Because *kich'im* is spontaneous, it is different from the knock which results from something like distrust of one's counterpart. One may release *kich'im* by accident, and there is no need to blush. Its reflection is just the same. It is not followed by such a direct and impetuous an answer as the "come in" or *entre* which you give to the sound of a knock; it reflects a more subtle method.

By stirring our bodies we let people know our presence by the indistinct sound of rustling clothes; then we move and the *ondol* paper on which we sit makes a sound. These are subtle signs meaning "I have heard your cough. It is proper for you to enter." This is a difference between the Occident and Korea. Without speaking to each other, we employ a subtle gesture and a suggestion from heart to heart which avoids directness. It is a subtle form of communication which indicates the Korean mind in much the same way as the half-open nature of the Korean stone wall which allows us to see inside but not too completely.[1]

The Korean mind is half open and half closed, like the father-in-law who says "ahem" so as not to embarrass his newly married daughter-in-law as he passes in front of the door of the guest room where she is staying quietly. Such consideration is subtle and as quiet as the surface of a lake at night.

When Westerners are happy, they hug and kiss each other. They can't write a letter without using "my dear" as a salutation for their father or mother or children. But Koreans never write "my dear" before the word "mother." Moreover, we don't use an overt expression of affection such as hugging and kissing. We stand face to face without expression. We transmit our feelings deeply and silently like pantomime actors with eyes ... lips ... trembling hands.

When the famous Silla general Kim Yu-shin (金庾信) was leading his troops and passed by his native village, he did just this. There was the house in which he was born. If he had only run and knocked at the door, he could have seen the face of his aged mother for whom he had yearned. But General Kim just let his soldiers go to his house and bring out black bean sauce. He stayed on his horse and tasted it. When he knew that the taste of the sauce was just the same as it always had been, he believed that his old mother was alright. General Kim mutely left and his

1. See Chapter 11.

52

mother must have shed tears as she hid on the wooden floor behind a window and looked at her son's manly appearance as he passed by.

This was a meeting and a departure from which only the sound of a cough remained. We have never viewed such a scene in a movie where a cowboy appears and knocks loudly at the door.

Boeyoong 67

13. Kim Yu-shin and Napoleon

KIM YU-SHIN (595–673A.D.) is our hero who unified
the Three Kingdoms in 638 A.D. He is the symbol of
the knightly order of *Hwarang* and is Korea's foremost
model of the military man.

But when we compare his actions with those of Napoleon, we discern in them the limited nature of the
"Korean hero." There are many differences between it
and the concept of the Western hero.

Napoleon came from the decayed Corsican nobility and, from a mere artillery officer, became Emperor. He was not a man who fitted himself to reality, but rather he was a hero who fought against convention and fitted reality to himself. But Kim Yu-shin obediently followed reality. In doing this he acted in a manner no different from other people. However much we think about it, he was in some degree cowardly.

Like Napoleon, Yu-shin was also descended from declining nobility—the Kaya kings. But he knew he never had a chance of success because in the strict Silla system of royal lineage he was not of pure blood.

Yu-shin did not try to break this kind of reality; he was a person who tried to fit himself to the system. Finally he made his own ambitious way by using his own sister in connection with Kim Ch'un-ch'u of the Silla royal house.

Kim Ch'un-ch'u already had a wife and children. Though this was the case, Yu-shin made a liaison between him and his young sister Munhi. He put Kim Ch'un-ch'u in Munhi's room, using as an excuse the need to patch Ch'un-ch'u's sleeve which had been torn in a game of football. Yu-shin prepared matters and quietly left the room.

So the virgin Munhi immorally conceived a child without being married. Yu-shin quickly used this situation and made his sister, Munhi, Kim Ch'un-ch'u's legal wife. We get goose pimples to think about it. We see not only Yu-shin's heroic appearance but the secret smile of a schemer like Iago. It is dirty and immoral.

No matter how great his ambition to unify the Three Kingdoms, we cannot rationalize Yu-shin's action in breaking up Kim Ch'un-ch'u's family and using the youth of his sister. How could we dare call this manly fair play?

Secondly, when an assassin appeared and tried to kill Napoleon, Napoleon caught him but didn't kill him. Rather, Napoleon gave the assassin a weapon and told him to try to kill him. They say that the would-be assassin ran away without being able to even touch Napoleon. Western knighthood is reflected in this episode.

But it is said that Yu-shin, who was a member of the *Hwarang*, or Korean knights, ordered the death of a Koguryŏ assassin named Paeksŏk, who had tried to kill him. Moreover, though Paeksŏk confessed that he would not harm Yu-shin and frankly and willingly said that he was an assassin sent by Koguryŏ, Yu-shin finally had Paeksŏk executed because he felt apprehensive. Wasn't the hero Yu-shin petty minded?

Thirdly, when Napoleon saw that a mirror broke while he was campaigning, he thought that something bad happened to Josephine and he withdrew his troops and went home. He was a hero who could conquer the world while he loved a woman.

But Yu-shin cut the throat of his horse who had taken him through habit (as Yu-shin was drunk at the time and the horse knew the way) to the house of the *kisaeng* Ch'ŏngwannyŏ to prevent this happening again after he had sworn never to visit her. For his dream of unification of the Three Kingdoms, the hero was one who had to sacrifice his love for the *kisaeng* Ch'ŏngwannyŏ. The hero believed that it would be difficult to unify the Three Kingdoms without giving up Ch'ŏngwannyŏ and forcing on her the loneliness of a solitary and empty home. Also he thought unification would be difficult without asking for troops from the T'ang Dynasty of China.

More than a lack of power, his attitudes and his way of thinking make us feel the so-called "Koreanish" destiny.

Fourth, while Napoleon viewed the dark sea of the lonely island of St. Helena, he died. The hero had to be tragic. Napoleon led vast armies and though he was about five feet tall he made the world tremble, and the curtain came down on his sorrowful death which was a history of fighting against fate.

But Kim Yu-shin, as a loyal official of the country, died quietly as an old man—the guardian protector of the nation. He was a person who lived his destined life. We are not trying to judge Kim Yu-shin in comparison with Napoleon. The concept of the hero is different. The Western hero emits a somewhat tragic odor. As he appears from the back, vaulting the wall of fate and fighting fiercely, the shadow of ruination is present as at the setting of the sun. They are people who live in opposition to men's lives. So the Western hero has a destiny of rebellion and destruction. A happy ending is not the world of the hero. The Western hero is burned out and is destroyed and then leaves behind a handful of ashes and disappears. They are people who choose their own fate.

But the Korean hero is one who is obedient and quietly follows and is in harmony with fate. He is a hero who is plain and normal more than bitter. There are no adventures beyond the horizon; he fights within his horizons. The hero does not vault his actual situation. He conforms to it.

Baeyoong 67

14. Dictatorship and *Arirang*

ONE cannot boast to others of crying at the movies even though one may be quite naive. Even more, not a few would scorn you if you cried seeing news features put out by the Ministry of Public Information which are certainly not tragedies.

But I daresay that I shed hot tears on seeing a news scene which was only a trifle and just a few tens of seconds long. It was the World Vision Children's chorus. I seem to remember that it was a ceremonial visit to the presidential mansion on completion of an American concert tour.

In America they got some donations of money and goods and they received much sympathy from a group called the Descendants of the Mayflower.

The children were born in a poor country and they also carry the burden of being war orphans. They sang *Arirang* innocently with such lovely lips. The sad tune tore at my heart. It was the flowing stream of a plaintive song which has appealed to us for a thousand years.

Of course, it was not because the song was sung by motherless children nor because *Arirang* is so sad that I shed tears sentimentally. The sadness welled up inside me in a moment when the scene of the fully white-haired President Syngman Rhee appeared against the background of the faces of the children's chorus.

In the wrinkled face of the 80-year-old aged President there was a lonely shadow which you find in a dictator. By the side of Francesca, his wife, he stood staring vacantly, eyes blinking, listening to the children sing *Arirang*.

"You old despot! What are you thinking about now? People respect you as the father of the country and follow you as they would their old father. We were trying to sing before you like pampered children. But you . . . oh, you."

My emotion isn't simply hate. We feel sorrow, regret and emptiness. If he were only younger, and if he were a little more heroic, and if it weren't a chorus of orphans returned from an American tour, and if they weren't just singing *Arirang*, and if only we were less unhappy in our old days, and if the Liberal Party weren't so tyranous — even without mentioning all these things, if he had been

59

a real dictator like Hitler, I then would not have shed such unbecoming tears but I might have angrily raised my fist at him.

Syngman Rhee wasn't a dictator who rode in an open car and appeared before public rallies. He was not a Hitler who screamed through his *Mein Kampf* and declared that he himself was a dictator under the banner of the swastika. He was not able to tread the path of complete dictatorship. Our old dictator didn't set fire to the Reichstag, he didn't abolish election regulations, and he didn't openly have storm troopers around him. But there was no difference between what he did and setting fire to the National Assembly, and it was the same as abolishing election regulations, and his police were like the storm troopers. The fact is he was a dictator who was negative. He was neither this nor that. He was only an inbetween grey dictator. So we couldn't hate him completely. Rather we felt a kind of sadness near to regret. Finally, Syngman Rhee was a Korean, in spite of his foreign wife and foreign training.

As I have indicated in my essay "The Meaning of Stone Walls," our culture sprung out from middle walls which were not completely open nor completely closed. The essence of the Korean mind is this vague semi-transparency, neither hot nor cold, and neither bright nor dim.

So we had no tyrant like Nero and no dictator like Hitler. We lack thoroughness and frankness and transparency. So there cannot ever be a distinct boundary.

When this half-openness and semi-transparency is applied in art and in emotion, and is like the sound of *kich' im* or the melody of *Arirang*, it emits a dim and pleasant scent. But when it enters politics and reality, it produces a senility of evil and hypocricy, with scheming, bad policies, negative chronic aggression and Syngman Rhee's dictatorship disguised as democracy.

So while *Arirang*, or Korea, and Syngman Rhee, with his foreign influences, seem heterogeneous, actually these are two flowers which have bloomed from the same root.

It was not a burning flame, nor was it completely extinguished; such dictatorial rule which burned fitfully was not only the characteristic trait of the period of Syngman Rhee. The Korean emotion, or this indistinctness, is a two-faced Janus which can be evil while being good. It was not positive strife, but the negative and hazy struggles of the long Yi Dynasty factional disputes which used all sorts of evil tricks as props in the dirty political struggles which evolved.

How many tyrants have there been who were not real tyrants but who have behind the scenes bruised the hearts of the people in some vague way! Yŏnsan was no Nero, Kim Yu-shin was no Napoleon, and Syngman Rhee was no Hitler. This land had no complete tyrants, heroes or dictators. They cannot be extinguished because they never really burned. This is the dim and tolerant nature which scholars have usually insisted upon as a Korean trait.

Bae Yoong 67

15. The Fighting of the Superior Man

Translator's note: The term "superior man" (君子 *kun-ja*) is taken from the Chinese Confucian classics. It generally means one who is superior in moral virtues, not in strength. It has sometimes been translated as "gentleman," but this has other connotations in English. I have preferred to use the term originally coined in a translation of the "Analects of Confucius."

A Japanese writer has described Korean fighting as follows: "Korean fighting is very different from that of the Japanese. First, they smoke a long bamboo pipe and engage in verbal wrestling with great fluency for thirty minutes or an hour without stopping. But this fight, which is one of staring and yelling, does not easily expand to involve fisticuffs. It is a fight of glaring, of rolling up

62

one's sleeves, of spittle flying, of pushing and of posturing as if they were going to fence. It is like a cat fight.

"If it becomes a little more extreme, while there may be some twisting of collars, most of them end with just pushing. We would have to look hard to find a fistfight.

"Naturally onlookers crowd around them. They leisurely smoke their pipes and ask each other for a light, and as if they were watching a drama, they listen carefully to the issues presented by both sides. Not only that, each fighter yells his side of the story to the audience and hints at asking for criticism of his opponent and sympathy for himself. When one somehow has grabbed the other's collar, some reconciler steps in, and then the yelling and the gestures suddenly become more vigorous, capitalizing on the reconciler as a neutral zone. All in all, the fighting of the Koreans is the fighting of the 'superior man.'"

As we might expect, this is a Japanese viewpoint. They have only seen the fights of the rash Tokyo-born men and the *samurai* in which people's necks are cut like the bottoms of cabbages, where daggers are used more than words and blood instead of spittle. So surely it is not unreasonable for them to think it strange to see a fight scene which is fought leisurely while long bamboo pipes are lit.

If our fight is like a catfight, the Japanese fights are just like cockfights. They are quick to start and quick to end. They are struggles in which blood always flows and in which victory and defeat are quite distinct. The fighters don't mind the viewers. The fight is already over when crowds gather around. Like an autumn squall, it is quickly over. With an "I surrender" the end is clear and the loser is vanquished and the winner victorious. They call this kind of fight "clear cut," but it is also cruel.

The fighting of Westerners is similar. Their fights are duels. It is a fight to the death. Their fights don't just make the sound of thunder, as do ours; they are fights of windswept storms with the smell of blood.

The custom of shaking hands proves this. As is widely believed, it is clear that this was a custom derived from the Middle Ages. Shaking hands is a kind of military disarmament. There is no need to worry about the other party's sword or pistol when he takes the other person's extended hand. So the extending of the right hand which holds the weapon is a kind of etiquette which means the greatest favor and affection. When shaking hands, putting forth the left hand or putting one hand in the pocket is thought to be a great breach of courtesy.

Because there are those who are expert pistol shots with their left hand, they feel uneasy extending only the right hand and so this has given rise among the insecure to the custom of shaking hands with both hands.

Finally, their fights are ones in which the use of fists or swords or pistols must follow. So we can't say that their fights are lukewarm like ours.

If we compare our fights with those of the Westerner, ours are ones in which we smoke and think about the effect on the viewers. They last a long time and we never use our fists except to point and to make dramatic gestures; so it is no lie to say that our people are a peaceful people.

But should we be glad because we have no barbarous custom of dueling? Though we call our fights those of the "superior man," if you are going to fight, how about finishing it off in a single breath rather than spending a lifetime glaring at each other and being lukewarm about it? Isn't it better to decide a fight by one's own strength rather than watching the attitudes of the onlookers? Isn't it true that because of war there can be peace and sometimes for peace there must be war? Isn't our armistice today a case of neither war nor peace? The rainy season of intermittent drizzle is the Korean atmosphere.

Since Japanese historical movies and Western drama were introduced here, this "fighting of the superior man" has somewhat changed. They have produced speed, thrills and intensity. Now in some rural areas you can't see our old kind of fights where each side grabs the other's collar and keeps that pose until sunset. It is not now a case of "I will kill you" in words, but of fights which end in blood. When we see children's fights they are pretty good imitations of Western movies.

But we can neither lament nor applaud to see that as times change, our fights, which used to be charming with leisurely drawing upon the long bamboo pipes and pointing and yelling, are now tougher. Although our nature has become much clearer and more distinct, we have also become so much more cruel. When I see this changing pattern of our fights I cannot easily judge whether it is good or bad. Can I say that this indecision is itself part of my "Koreanish" nature?

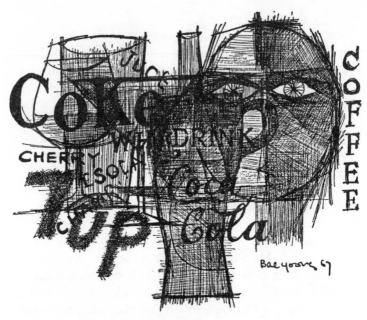

16. On Beverages and Culture

Translator's note: Scorched rice tea, called *sung nyung* (숭늉), is a drink made from the scorched rice remaining on the bottom of the pot in which rice was cooked. It is mixed with hot water and thus becomes lukewarm. It is drunk following a meal. *Makkŏli* is a rather mildly alcoholic, fermented rice drink, often made at home in rural areas. *Sujŏnggwa* (수정과) is a drink made from sugared water in which dried persimmons and ginger have been placed.

EACH time I drink Coca-Cola, I think about American civilization. The dark red color is like rusted steel. It has a taste somewhat bitter and tangy, and something in it, which never has the reverberations of an aftertaste, seems like the belch of a capitalist civilization. In it is the vigor of cowboys running over the blue Texas plains. Mixed together in it is also the pungent and prosaic special taste of the smoke of the Chicago factory chimneys and the muddy Mississippi. It has a sense of taste both busy and vacant.

As Buess, the history of civilizations writer, has confessed, "To the eye of a writer landing in Bangkok looking for Thai curios, the first scene that one sees is Coca-Cola piled high in trucks." It is not only the taste of the cola, but also the image of the can which is a symbol of all the economic strength of American civilization.

It seems that in a country's beverages there lie hidden the true secrets of that civilization. In the red and transparent wine is the clever French intellectual and the pure luxury of the fountains of Versailles; in beer is German romance and, like the foam, the ideal flourishes and is then extinguished. In astringent black tea is English realism, while its smell contrasts with the mysterious fragrance of the tea leaves which is the dream of the Orient.

Likewise, they say that Korean taste lies in scorched rice tea. Whenever I drink it for breakfast or dinner, I feel Korea. Its color is like the indistinct tone of Korean *ondol* paper. It is such an appetizing taste. It seems that while it has color, it really has no color, and while it has a taste, it really hasn't. One can know the taste after one drinks it and one can see the color only after it is poured. An indistinct taste lingers on the lips. In the scorched rice tea are the blunt yet emotion-filled sound of the cough of the grandfather and the kind touch of the maternal grandmother, the sound of the *kŏmunko* of the Silla Dynasty musician U Rŭk, and the musical sounds of the moving of the clothes of Ch'unhyang. The lukewarm sense of scorched rice tea, neither hot nor cold, is the body temperature of the Korean.

But what about *makkŏli*? It isn't strong like whiskey or Chinese vodka. And it isn't transparent. In *makkŏli*, which is opaque, astringent and bland, is the Korean loneliness like the humor of the wandering Yi Dynasty poet Kim Sat-kat. The thick and disagreeable taste of *makkŏli* is the Korean's sentiment and demure romantic spirit. So in scorched rice tea and *makkŏli* together is the irony of a "character without any character." They are not like Coca-Cola, wine and beer. Actually it is difficult to say that they have a taste.

If there is a taste to scorched rice tea and *makkŏli*, it is a paradoxical sense of taste which must be called a "taste without a taste." It is the feeling of the hermit who does nothing but lives his whole life plainly. That is, the feeling is as some poet wrote, "If asked why I live on, I would laugh," and it is a strange emotion of detachment, resignation and self-comfort. Perhaps if Korean tears and laughter were put together to form one liquid, no doubt it would be like scorched rice tea or *makkŏli*. Also in scorched rice tea and *makkŏli* there are no man-made tastes. They are natural; they are neither embellished nor pretentious. They are produced just as they are, and the taste may be brash but never base.

As in the saying "If it is not transparent, it is not French," the French love intellect which is clear, rational and distinct. But in our case, it is quite the opposite and

68

it may be said "If it is not opaque, it is not Korean." We like emotions which are rather hazy and simple and which cannot be distinctly separated. We have lived being and yet not being, living and yet not living. Like scorched rice tea, our lives are neither hot nor cold. Our history is like *makkŏli*, neither wine nor water; it continues to eternity like the reverberations of a bell, reverberations which no one can take away. From our stone walls which are seen and yet half-seen to the taste of the scorched rice tea which exists and yet doesn't exist, our emotions flow in this way in everything Korean.

We have lived for several thousand years in the corner of a vast mainland. As we have had to live being poor, there was no luxurious disguise, and as we always had to live in oppression, we have not been able to expose ourselves openly. If we were to overcome these many hardships and suffering, we had to live with our roots in dimness like these reverberations.

So while we emit passion, we are restrained, and while we cry, we smile, and while we obey, we rebel, and we had to look at the *nunch'i* of others while trying to keep our own land. From such a life a taste like scorched rice tea is produced.

This is the only place where our people can stay; it is an in-between and grey neutral area. In it they tried to live better and refine their emotions.

So like the gloomy thatched roofs of the village huts where suddenly there may be seen red peppers spread out to dry, sometimes the scorched rice tea is changed to the taste of a refined and very refreshing beverage like a *sujŏnggwa.*

FASHION

17. On Clothes

LIKE Carlyle, the Chinese philosopher Lin Yu-t'ang wrote two articles with somewhat pretentious titles such as "The Philosophy of Clothes" and "A Rational Essay on Clothes." He insisted that "when men and women take off their clothes, they seem to resemble monkeys more than anything else and the more they wear them the more they make asses out of themselves." It seems he thought that only when clothes are worn properly will the light finally dawn.

Therefore, Lin Yu-t'ang never could show respect for ladies in the social whirl who covered their necks with collars over seven centimeters high when the temperature was over 100 degrees. The main reason for Lin Yu-t'ang's attack on the defects of Western clothing as unnatural and inhuman was the unnatural collar and the dog-collar, or necktie.

The collar interferes with man's profound thought and wholehearted deliberation, and the trouser belt causes indigestion. Therefore, he finally came to the conclusion that he chose Chinese clothes above Western clothes.

If this is the case, what about our Korean clothes? We must for a moment here discuss the Korean "philosophy of clothes." Nothing has a more direct link to life than clothes, and nothing demonstrates the national traits of a people better than their clothes. It is essential to note that the history of Korean clothes symbolizes the history of our people's lives. We must understand that Korean clothes, like so many things in our culture, have been subjected to strong influences from abroad.

During the Paekche and Silla periods we wore a flowing robe until the time when the influence of the Chinese Dynasty of T'ang swept over our land. We divided our clothes, argue some specialists, into an upper part (the *chŏgori*) and the lower part (the *ch'ima*) in accordance with the T'ang style.

Under the Mongol domination, in imitation of the Mongol and Chinese clothes, the width of the Koryŏ man's pants and the Koryŏ woman's upper sleeves became narrower.

In the Yi Dynasty, the influence of Ming China became predominant.

In the thirty-first year of King Chungjong (1536),

the court ordered the people to imitate directly the Ming costume. But before, in the tenth year of King Sejo (1465), Kim Su, the magistrate of Kwangju-Gun in Kyŏnggi Province, memorialized the throne: "Our system has imitated things Chinese, but only women's ornaments and clothes follow the old practice; so I therefore humbly suggest that we ask the royal dieticians and the interpreters to teach the unmarried nurses and the *kisaeng* at court the Ming style of costume."

And then at the close of the Yi Dynasty, when Western influence was rampant on the Chinese mainland, the clothing style of court officials began to change to the Western fashion. At the time of the 1884 reform, when Kim Ok-kyun and Pak Yŏng-hyo sought political asylum in Japan, the common people began to wear Western clothes.

Korean clothes are just the same as our Korean history of misfortune. This is obvious if we recall the uniform called "national clothes" and the women's trousers which Koreans were forced to wear during the Japanese colonial period. Today in the street are the "mambo-pants," the sack dress and the bikini.

The unparalleled changes in fashions and modes reflect the turbulent ups and downs of our history.

Nevertheless, it is astonishing to me that we still preserve our unique traditional clothes which are different from the Chinese and the Western.

Our clothes retain a secret akin to a miracle, of having been able to preserve our own language and way of life in spite of countless oppressions and aggressions. Under waves of overpowering foreign strength, nobody can deny our people's wisdom which enabled them to keep their identity.

Superficially, we appear to have been one hundred percent assimilated by foreign powers. But what constitutes the undercurrent of Korean history is nothing but the spirit of the nation, the spirit of the Korean people.

Although sunshine has not always shone through and development has not leapt forward under continuous pressure, this spirit reminds us of the noble image of an old stone pagoda which has withstood the wind and rain. The style of the Korean costume, which has withstood various hardships and persecutions, is the crystallization of the Korean mind, made of blood and tears, amidst this turbulent history.

Officials have not ordered this, nor have our leaders or intellectuals asked us to do so. Moreover, we have not had such wonderful designers as Dior. Rather, they have forced us to wear the clothes of the Mongols, the Chinese or other foreigners.

What have made the Korean clothes of today are our earth and our wind. Our hearts are like the village women who lived their simple lives attached to earth and the woodcutters who sang beating on the legs of the A-frame while looking up at the clear blue sky.

The sad story of our history is written in the cuffs of our blouse and in each pleat of our skirt.

On our stained collar there is a breath of exhaustion and in the broken string of hemp sandals, in the worn-out tips of our turned-up white socks, or in the thoughtlessly moving ribbons of our blouses, there is the wishful prayer of the common people who have lived waiting for a thousand years.

18. Spread Your Wings

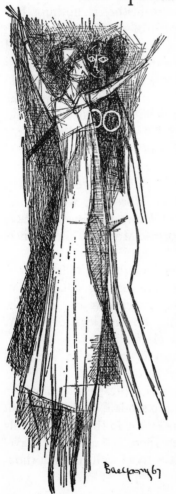

Baechong 67

A proverb of ours says "Clothes like at a wedding, and food like the autumnal feast of *Ch'usŏk.*" By these words we mean we always want to dress as well as when we are to be married and to eat at any time the way we feast at *Ch'usŏk.*

Although other countries may have similar thoughts, in our case, where there has not been enough to live on, we can assume that this has been an especially great concern. Also in our country the ideal of the most beautiful life is "wearing a skirt twelve panels wide and walking in a room six measures large."

It seems that Korean beauty clearly lies in Korean clothes. If we were to use more specialized terminology, our clothes form a harmony of the ideal, mixing those of the northern, or closed kind, with the southern, or open style.

The beauty of clothes is that they reveal the body while hiding it, and this is especially true of women's clothes. In ancient days they wore the robe in the West and in Japan, the *kimono*. In comparison with Korean clothes they give a feeling of being unnatural and too complicated. They say that these clothes destroy the body line. You don't see the people first, but rather the clothes.

The special attraction of the Japanese women wearing *kimonos* is their exposed white neck, and in the West it is considered beautiful when women bare their breasts. There is a contrast between the revealing of one's skin, which is beauty of the body, and the beauty of clothes which cover the body. So clothes emphasizing the beauty of the body, like the bikini of today, were developed, but they weren't necessarily for swimming. There is no difference between this and Eve covering her shame with a leaf. If men are to admire the beauty of the body, the beauty of clothes must die, and if we want the beauty of clothes, body beauty will wither away. Isn't this the tragedy of Western clothes?

But in the case of Korea, the beauty of clothes and the body are not separate but form together a final unified beauty.

In support of this argument, suppose you take off Western clothes. The clothes by themselves have a three dimensional nature. But if you take off Korean clothes, they become nothing but a single cloth. So Western clothes are hung on hangers and Korean clothes are put away folded.

Korean clothes have their special characteristics in

nature. Also, the body is neither completely exposed nor is it completely hidden. The thin ramie blouse worn in summer dimly and half-transparently reveals the elasticity of the fresh body. The flowing line of the skirt around the waist is just the same.

> *Inside the ramie blouse*
> *Her breast like a rounded white porcelain water*
>   *dropper.*
> *If you look too much, you will suffer,*
> *So take a single glance!*

The sensuality of Korean clothes, which is illustrated in this farmer's song sung while planting rice, is not clearly distinguishable like the bikini, but rather shows its most wonderful attraction in its impatience which is still subdued.

Moreover, between the short blouse and the skirt, at times a little white skin shows under the arm. This is evident in the paintings of Tan Wŏn (1760–?). In "Treatise of Sŏngho" (星湖僿說), the people in the olden days called it "clothes provocation."

The simple nature of the Korean skirt and blouse is difficult to find in other countries of the world. It has none of the lousy attachments of the *kimono*.

Rather, Korean women's clothes have a subtle sex appeal. Their simplicity and the extraordinarily light movement of the line are their aesthetic traits.

When Westerners dress up, they say that it is "beautiful," but when we see the same thing we express our pleasure by calling it "chic" (lit. slender 날씬하다) or "nice" (lit. flying 날아 갈듯하다).

Chŏng Ch'ŏl in one of his *sijo* poems expressed it:

All day washing and rewashing blouses
Dry, dry them in the bright sun, and iron them.
Look at it hanging on such a soaring feathery
   shoulder.

That's so. The blouse is light and it hangs on the shoulder like flying butterfly wings. The long blouse ribbons flying in the wind are so graceful too. The bows are not used only for practical purposes, like buttons. After tying, there still remains a long ribbon, and it gives a feeling of such delicate movement that the image it evokes is of fairies flying into the heavens. Though the Western angel has wings, the Oriental angel has replaced wings with the fluttering and moving of clothes in rhythm. It gives a stronger image of flying than do wings. So we can see the Korean blouse ribbon and the skirt as a kind of wings, in which we put aside reality and dream of the blueness of an exciting sky. So the proverb "Clothes are wings" is not a chance expression.

Our impulse has been to try to fly to everlasting heaven to break the fetters of the earth which is full of the tears of living with in-laws, the bitter farewells with our lovers, and chastity cruelly trapped under the aggression of foreign enemies. And it has been a painful longing which has settled into Korean clothes. It is clothing of escape.

The many-folded wide skirt of the Western woman is pulled by gravity down towards solid ground; but the light line of the Korean women's slender skirt and the tightly bound blouse look ready to fly upwards to the sky when the wind blows.

The hearts of our women who had to live without

freedom in such hardship must have wanted to fly skyward like a bird or a butterfly. Unconsciously, this latent and unusual will has finally come out in the flying blouse and skirt; and these clothes may have shielded their wounds.

Bae yoong 67

19. Korean Pants and
Western Trousers

NOT all the special characteristics of Korean pants are good. From another angle, we can say that there hasn't been much change in these clothes. In fact, I don't have the courage to praise these pants however much I examine them. Even though it may be rude to say so, when I think of the appearance of our ancestors who fought wearing these baggy pants, I can't help laughing. I wonder how they were able to fight such swift foreign enemies, and not just once or twice, wearing such loose and baggy clothes.

When we look at the tights of the men of the age

of Napoleon, the trousers were close-fitting like stockings or knitted underwear. The pants of the cowboys in Western movies are also the same. If we had had such clothes we too might have had the ambition to conquer the world.

Korean pants fit everyone alike, and it is difficult to distinguish which is the front and which is the back, and which belongs to Mr. Pak, and which is Mr. Kim's. Even when a well-built man fools around with wearing Korean pants one cannot help saying that he looks like a moron and that they just don't fit. These pants are clothes which are more fit to sitting in the warm corner of the ondol floor and reciting the old classics... "Confucius said... Mencius said...." They are clearly not clothes for action.

In ancient days both men and women generally wore skirts. In Greek and Roman times they both wore clothes much like a nightgown. In Japan today a men's skirt, called a *hakama*, is worn. The Scottish army uniform is also skirt-like.

So some will ask that since in some countries men wear skirts, in comparison aren't our baggy pants more useful for action?

But you must not forget that the point is, however short the skirt, it is easier to move the body in it than in baggy pants. Isn't the special trait of Korean pants that they are wide and indistinct compared with trousers?

Secondly, if we term Western clothes a solid, Korean clothes (and Oriental clothes are also similar) are a plane. Everyone says that the collar and the crease of Western trousers give the impression of being a solid; but Korean pants give a flat feeling.

While Western clothes can be explained as unnatural and Korean clothes as more natural, it is also logical to say that Western clothes give a three dimensional impression and our clothes give the feeling of being two dimensional. Not only clothes, but Western culture is a solid while Korean culture can be seen as a plane. A solid means space. They knew how to use space and they built buildings and airplanes. We didn't have such things.

Thirdly, Korean pants don't have pockets. Although it seems that having pockets or not is a very simple matter, here there is already a gap between scientific and non-scientific thinking. Our ancestors did not think of making pockets in our clothes (and those in Korean vests today are a modern innovation). They made and carried a separate bag for this purpose.

I suppose the Korean word "pocket" (호주머니) comes from the Mongol, as we call them "Mongol" or "savage" pockets indicating that they came from that neighboring country. From the origin of the word I must conclude in the final analysis that pockets were not a Korean invention.

So while we carried a bag in the folds of our pants in which we put our flint, the Westerners simply put their belongings into their pockets. Korean pants may thus be seen to be unscientific compared with trousers.

Fourthly, in our country underpants or underwear did not exist. Outside the jacket we wore a vest and over the vest an overcoat, so although we developed an established pattern for some of our clothes, we wore pants over our naked bodies. Today there is still no difference from the old days in this custom. So it is important to note that underclothes were not developed.

Of course, in the case of women's clothes, there was something which we call underwear (단속옷) in Korea and *kosimaki* in Japan. But when we consider the Korean situation, we only thought of clothes as an outside decoration. The fact that inner clothes didn't exist may be said to indicate a lack of substance.

Of course there is a relationship here to economic factors, but since we had overcoats why didn't we make underwear which needed only the size of a cloth for wrapping parcels? Why did such a moral-minded people not think of making underclothes?

Accordingly, the kinds of clothes we have are quite poor. But when we examine the many kinds of Western clothes which are worn according to different times and occasions, such as morning clothes, afternoon clothes, evening wear, party and cocktail dresses, etc., our clothes in comparison just won't do.

In Korea we didn't even have pajamas.

20. Are Korean Clothes White?

It is said that Koreans like white clothes. From the ancient Puyŏ era this custom has come down to us. Furthermore this has given rise to the expression that the Koreans are "the white clothed people." Why was white picked among so many colors? Have we really liked the color white? It seems that it will never be easy to understand this emotion and to find the origins of this custom, so there are many guesses.

Some say the white color symbolizes sunlight. Because our people worshiped the sun as a god and believed themselves to be the offspring of the sun, it is said that they made the color of their clothes the holy color, white.

There are also some who say that if you read the old text of the "Collection of Essays" by Chipong (芝峰類說), you will find it says that after the reign of King Myŏngchong (明宗) we wore white because national mourning took place continuously. Each time there was a national mourning for some royal personage, the people had to put on white mourning clothes. This continued for a long time and became firmly established as a custom.

Some see it differently. They look on it as a Yüan Dynasty custom. They wore white clothes. When the Yüan ruled Koryŏ, didn't the whole court follow Yüan customs? As the king's food was called by the Yüan name of *sura*, the clothes color simply followed that of the Yüan as well. So during the Koryŏ period the farmers wore white ramie cloth. But the discussion isn't over yet.

Others say it is quite different. They should not examine this problem from the viewpoint of religious ceremony or social ceremony or from political reasons. Some say that you have to take into account the socio-economic aspects as well. In the Yi Dynasty "Essays of P'ilwŏn" (筆苑雜記) the fact is noted that there was a lack of dyeing materials. Dyeing was not developed and also there was no time for such processing. They were busy enough living by spinning thread from cotton and making cloth which they wore in its original color, white. The theory is that if the natural color of cotton were red, we would have been known as the red-clothed people, and if black, the black-clothed people.

But I suppose there are still others who might add to these views and some who would refute them saying that the lack of the development of dyeing means no interest in color. Basically the color of clothes arises from the stimulation of human sexual desire. Take a look at the beautiful feathers of the peacock and the bird of paradise. But in Korea relations between the sexes were completely severed and they weren't especially anxious about the color of clothes. When we think about it, we understand why the *kisaeng* and the new bride didn't wear white but wore varied colors.

We cannot say that the Koreans liked white for its own sake even though they wore nothing but white; but if you think about it more deeply, it was because our sense of the beauty of the color of clothes had been dulled.

On the other hand, others argue pointing out the saying "If it is the same price, buy a crimson skirt." The king and the court ladies didn't wear white, did they?

There are those who would shake their heads and deny this saying it is not like this at all. The white color must match the faces of the Koreans and the climate and nature. Rather, we wore white because our sense of the beauty of color was refined. The Chinese who live in the yellow earth wear dark blue which fits their situation, and for the Koreans, the clear blue sky creates a beautiful harmony with white.

We have established many hypotheses on the origins of white clothes. But in the strictly objective sense we could point out that white is not a color. And the fact is that it arose from poverty. We must look at our white clothes from these two viewpoints.

We say white clothes, and it is not too negative to say that it is a natural color. Our talk on the character of white clothes is "We wore clothes without dyeing them." The sense of the color of the cotton, the hemp, and the ramie clothes is different. It was not their hope to make that color — there was no other way but to follow the given natural color of the material. We have lived following along our given fate and our ancestors simply accepted white.

Because of poverty there was no dyeing, and Korea's secret lies in that, instead of saying she adapted herself to these conditions. When Koreans think that there is no way to escape from the devil, then they try to love it. While they feel uneasy, it is not the wearing of white but the thought that they must love white which bothers them.

So, though they did have some dyeing, they have dyed their clothes a homely and demure blue.

At present, discontent has been restrained. But it is not simply restraint, but rather the restraint of the longing for beautiful colors; this means that the idea of the love of white is worthless.

There is no one to blame nor anything to boast about in our white clothes. Although it is clear that it was a color derived from poverty, we have been willing to wear this color.

In white clothes we can see the sad custom of adjusting ourselves to our condition and loving our fate.

21. The Theory of Hats

Translator's note: Hats have had an important place in Korea. Traditionally, they have been of many kinds. The upper-class Koreans, the *yangban* and officials, wore two hats: the outside hat was known as a *kat*(갓), and the inner hat, around the topknot, the *t'angŏn*(탄건). The common people wore what was called a *tugŏn*(두건) which, on the analogy of the handkerchief, might be translated as a "hat-kerchief."

For the upper-class man to be without a hat, even in the house, was unthinkable and a loss of face.

THERE is an old folksong which goes "Is loyalty treachery?" They say that this song was popular at the time when King Yŏnsan was deposed in 1506. If we translate this literally, it means loyalty actually was nothing but treachery. In it we laugh scornfully at the opportunistic court officials. But if we look into the origins of the saying, there is a more interesting meaning.

During the Yi Dynasty, palace officials all wore hats. And usually there was embroidered on the hats the word "loyalty." But while the officials formally wore the hat, they were actually thinking of various treacherous schemes.

As the sounds for the words "royal hat," *samo* (紗帽), and treachery, *samo* (詐謀), are the same, this has given rise to the ironic humor of the folksong "Is loyalty treachery?" We also say "a hat-wearing robber," and this proverb indicates the corruption of the government officials who wore a hat and at the same time engaged in acts of robbery. It is not put too strongly to say that at that time the hat was a symbol of power and a symbol of falseness.

It was so not only in court, but everyone liked to wear something on their heads. Although this has been true in other countries as well, our people seem to have a special fondness for wearing hats. Mr. Ch'oe Nam-sŏn once made this point. Although both the inner and the outer hat originally came from China, it was more fashionable in Korea than in China, and it is said that our skill in making hats was very highly developed. The method of construction was not with thread, but with human or horsetail hair. Furthermore, they were exported to China where the Chinese liked to use the "horsehair" hat. Actually, we were the chief of the hat-wearing countries.

We may translate the fact of liking to wear hats as

an indication of great etiquette. The Englishman has an especially great interest in hats. We may say that the English silk hat rivals that of the Korean. As E. H. Carr, the essayist, wrote, the silk hat of the English was a symbol of conservatism and status.

We have a proverb about meeting disgrace while wearing a hat, and in English humor they satirize the gentleman who runs hurriedly after his hat which the wind blew off. The English and the Koreans think that hats are very close to saving face. The hat makes the English gentleman and the Korean "superior man."

The English essayist Chesterton had a really original and satiric idea about hats. He said that on a very windy spring day on top of a hill there should be a ladies' and gentlemen's hat-catching contest. His opinion was that the sight of so many ladies and gentlemen awkwardly chasing their hats blown by the wind had the possibility of developing into a wonderful sport, and that many spectators would come to cheer them on.

Hats have the marvellous power of making ladies and gentlemen more dignified. So if one encounters a situation like the proverb "Wearing a hat and meeting disgrace," it is quite something. It seems that only a people who like to wear hats and know the dignity of hats can taste the nuance of this proverb.

Koreans have proof that we have more understanding of the nature of the dignity of hats than the English. This is because the English, however much they attach importance to hats, must take them off in the presence of seniors. This is a type of etiquette. But in Korea rather than taking them off, we have the dignified custom of keeping them firmly on. Even before the king we didn't take them off; we wore them while bowing deeply. So it seems that the Korean hat occupies a higher position than the silk hat of the English.

Moreover, we each wore two hats, so our people surely have the honor of being the world's first hat-loving people. This is because our ancestors wore an inner and an outer hat. Also, we treasured them so we tied them with strong string. There is no comparison between our case and a scene where an English gentleman loses his face and awkwardly chases his hat blown by the wind.

Their tying on of hats is limited to when they are in battle and wear helmets in a life or death situation. Also, our horsehair hats are so very light, and this proves that they are quite developed. We distinguish between married men and bachelors by whether they wear hats, and marriage is the most important ceremony throughout one's whole life. It seems that we clearly are a people who like to wear hats.

But although the love of wearing hats in this degree proves our high esteem of etiquette, on the other hand it also indicates our living by outward show and our custom of authoritarianism, formalism and conservatism.

We who live poorly only wear hats and spend money like drunken sailors. Today we still talk of aspiring to wear the hat of official office (감투) which is a meaningless consciousness of false etiquette.

Actually, is not the battle of today, which is that of struggle for the hat of officialdom (감투싸움), a vestige of our people who have loved hats? When we look at the inside of the empty hat we often sigh.

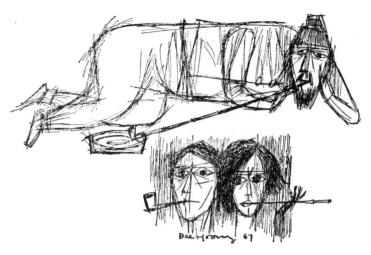

22. Regrets on the Long Bamboo Pipe

Translator's note: The Korean smoking-pipe stem is made from a thin elongated bamboo stalk with its joints opened. Its bowl is often of white brass. The Western pipe is usually called in Korea the "Madras Pipe," as it was associated with sailors, many of whom at that time were involved in the India-Far Eastern trade patterns.

WHEN we say "pipe" we think of the descendants of the Vikings with their broad chests covered with black bushy hair. Their masculine strength is expressed by their bronzed arms, tattooed with wriggling snakes and eagles, and their sea-wind-burned faces with traces of scars. It is the image of violence, adventure and action-packed vitality.

But when we say "the long bamboo pipe of the

Korean," we are reminded of an elderly gentleman lying for hours on the warm part of the guestroom *ondol* floor, the sound of coughing from his lips, the murmuring of lines of some poem in the classical language, his face blanched and yellowed resembling the color of *ondol* paper —an atmosphere of limitless weakness and dignity. There is a different feeling between puffing on the stubby Western pipe and puffing on the long, thin bamboo pipe.

Western pipe tobacco smells like the sea and seems to have a powerful movement like the muscles of youth. But the lazily uncoiling purple smoke from the long bamboo pipe is like the slender line of the four sages (iris, bamboo, plum and chrysanthemum) quietly pervading the cozy atmosphere of the screened guestroom. It is the smell of an old man. This comparison is drawn not only from simple imagination; it has reason, as the pipe has been elongated three feet since it was introduced into Korea.

The elderly gentlemen of this land are like plants; they lie vegetating and never rise. Their only action is smoking their long pipes. They don't stand up and move to perform the troublesome act of lighting the pipe bowl or getting an ash tray. They stretch out the long pipe while lying down and immediately pull an ash tray or any kind of furniture they need to them with the pipe. One who burns his eyelashes with a gas lighter is a child of the mechanical age; the Korean automatically lights his long pipe from the brazier while lying relaxed on the floor. The tobacco burns ten miles away. He doesn't worry about tobacco burning his hand or ashes in his eyes like those cigar smokers.

Although Westerners boast about making life automatic and replacing the button with the zipper, we still haven't heard the news of their inventing an automatic safety pipe. Long ago in the West, patients who entered the hospital suffering from burns must not have had the benefits of the long bamboo pipe as we had.

Not only that, but in the long pipe there was an authority holier than that in the staff of Aaron. In Korean society which respects the aged so much, the long pipe had a mysterious power. When a grandson was ill-behaved or when a rascal talked back saucily, all that was needed was for the grandfather to wave his three-foot-long pipe. Before the raised pipe touched the offender, he would run away astonished.

Although the long pipe was so convenient and had almost infinite power inside the house, outside in the street it was, as they say, a "useless, long thing."

Let's suppose that a gentleman gets on a crowded bus in the city with the long pipe, or let's think about the hunter or the man working quietly in an office calmly smoking one. How is it possible? So we have discovered the rule that pipe length is in inverse ratio to the amount of action required.

So the Korean pipe which was so long means, in effect, that we have lived our lives in laziness and enervation, in inactivity and asociality. So too it is an invention arising from a "house culture" not a "street culture" and from a "theory of sleep" rather than a "theory of action." It is clear that the long pipe was for the hermit, far from the world of action.

We have spent four thousand years lying down. After

the period of the Three Kingdoms, we always thought of spending our lives prone. Action has been consi..ered to be base.

Although the Korean words for action (질 and 짓) originally meant "movement," there is not one good word which is a combination of this word 질 with others. We are a people who subconsciously think that action equals baseness, as in such examples as "teaching" (先生질), "robbing" (도둑질), "fighting" (싸움질), "adultery by men" (오입질), "adultery by women" (화냥질), "kicking," (발짓) "pointing" (손짓), etc.

Although we admired music as a refinement of the arts, we have had contempt for drama as it involves action. And in our country this has been an important reason drama has not developed. We can see in this a deep reflection of the long pipe as one reason why drama was neglected in the old days and has decayed.

Likewise there is a relationship between the long pipe and Korean social stagnation. It is a symbol of a negative attitude towards action.

Nowadays the long bamboo pipe has simply become a vestige of the past, neither good nor bad. If there is one thing I am concerned about, it is whether the long pipe, symbol of the laziness and inactivity which dwelt in our minds, has really been broken.

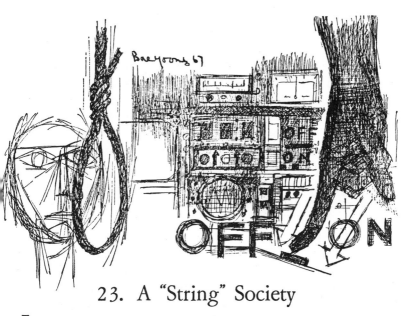

23. A "String" Society

IF Western society can be called a society of "buttons,"
Korea can be called a society of "strings."

In the West, there are buttons to press everywhere.
Elevators, refrigerators, washing machines, and all bells and
machines are operated by buttons. But someday the society
or culture which is built on buttons can also be destroyed
by buttons. By simply pressing a button the world can be
ended; all things can be changed into ashes by a button
called the "switch button" of a guided missile. Given this,
it is with reason that to the Westerner, pressing a button
means "a simple method producing a sequence of occur-
rences," or that "to button up" means "to make the last
agreement."

As Westerners control their society by means of buttons, Koreans have lived in the world in accordance with string. String is a symbol of Korea. From the strings on a Korean jacket to those on a horsehair hat, all connections are tied with string. The long, braided hair and ribbons are no exception. The string on the purse worn at the waist is so, and the strings tying the bottom of a man's trousers are the same, as are all ornaments. It is this string that makes our fate, and our history continues and is connected by the string of "your" and "my" karmas.

Visible and invisible strings have ruled us. So when people feel despair in loneliness, they say "the strings have become untied," and quite the reverse, they express the way a person has managed to survive by depending on something as "tying the string." The proverb which states that case is "The puppet has become untied," which means one has lost one's connection with another person. The expression "to be bound to something," in Korean, is composed of the words for string and tying. When something is stubborn and tough, we say that it is "tough like a string."

But in the West, the term "string" or "cord" has no especially good usage. If you say "string," it means a cumbersome "accessory condition," and also when you say "cord," it is used to mean "confinement" or the "punishment of hanging." Furthermore, the word "string" is not often used as a symbol of connection with others.

However, when we are connected with something, we use the term "to tie." We tie friendships and contracts, and we tie love. But if Westerners use the term "to tie," the meaning is to restrain and to interfere with the actions of others.

When we talk about marriage and loyalty, sometimes we use the term "to tie," and its nuance generally implies a connection close to fatal restraint. To have a relationship one doesn't use the term "tie" in the West, but the word "form." The usage of the word "tie" is a kind of comparison in which we feel the difference between Western and Korean societies. If buttons are independent and solid, string is always dependent and two dimensional, and is a kind of "line." Westerners see the relationships between people as form; we see ours as line, tied to each other as one string to another.

In general what does this tie mean for Koreans? It is my leaving myself in the hands of others, a unification of "you" and "me." Each of the two knotted strings loses its sense of independence. Neither "you" nor "I" exist but both become one string.

But in the West when A is joined to B like a heap of bricks, their form becomes another substance. Each one shows in unity the appearance of having preserved an independent nature. If we say that Korean society is like a spool of thread in which the string is all ravelled, then Western society is like an operating factory connected by buttons. Like ivy, string must depend on something. It must tie itself or be restrained by another. When the string breaks, it is destroyed. This is the tragic nature of line. But in the solid Western society, each individual's character freely makes contact with another independently. So theirs is a "unified society" and Korea is an "entangled society." Our history and society have been joined and sustained completely by string. Our society is one which has formed a line in which fathers and children, husbands and wives, and kings and officials, etc., are all entangled like one string with another.

Our society is one which has been handed down in relationships such as the one between grandfather and grandchild, so there has been no break or collision in our tradition. Though there are cases of it becoming unravelled or cut, our society does not have a history which has fallen apart. The tying of string on a one-to-one basis is most idealistic, but when there are three strings together they immediately become entangled. But the more buttons there are, the more stable and strong the whole becomes.

It is said that the more Koreans there are, the weaker they become, and that Koreans do not have a cooperative spirit. The reason could be that theirs is a relationship just like strings which become more ravelled and more complicated as they increase in number. In much the same way that wild vines become entangled, strife is bound to occur. We are not able to distinguish which one is "me" and which one is "you." In such circumstances, when relationships are disconnected, everything becomes all the more ravelled.

If we think about our human relationships or our political climate, we may be able to understand our social structure which is entwined like a string. The reformation of society requires a great deal of effort. If even one portion of this entangled mass is cut off, the social fabric will be destroyed.

Author's note: The theory of buttons is to make contact with one another and the theory of strings is to tangle with one another. Therefore, when we compare the origin of the word "conflict" in English and Korean, we can distinguish between Western and Oriental societies.

The word "conflict" originated from the Latin *confligere* which is the combination of *con* (together) and *fligere* (to strike). So "conflict" means contact and striking; but in Korean, "conflict"(葛藤) means that the arrowroot plant and wisteria vine are tangled together. Westerners looked at disharmony as striking each other, but Orientals thought of it as tangling with each other.

Bae young 67

24. Living in Togetherness

SOMETIMES in front of a counter in a Korean teahouse or restaurant an unusual sort of a fight takes place. It is one in which the participants take each other's hands and push them away and pull one another's clothes. Of course, there is some shouting too. But more strange is the fact that the people around never seem concerned. And this is not chaos resulting from trouble between the guest and the owner over paying the restaurant bill or counting the change. It is a quarrel between friends who only a little before were sitting together eating in quite a friendly manner. This fight never lasts more than one minute.

One of them pushes the other aside, and as he rushes from the counter, the curtain goes down on this strange wrestling match. Then the quarrelers leave the teahouse more intimately than when they were drinking together. The special characteristic of this fight is always that the one who has been defeated is more sorry than the victor. We cannot explain these fights as being due to our high-level sporting mentality. This is a scene which can never be explained in accordance with the foreigners' common-sense viewpoint.

But we Koreans know such fights very well. Everyone has experienced them. It is a quarrel as to who will pay for the tea, a "beautiful quarrel" and a "friendly fight." Are there any other people who have such an overly friendly fight? If we examine the customs of the selfish Westerners who eat together and yet pay separately, surely their practice is to us like the riddle of the sphinx.

Korean friendship is superior to material things. It is a fine custom of ours; a sort of beautiful morality which is more than a "friendship of trust" and beyond a "friendship of assistance."

Our proverb "With friends one does not mind going anywhere" is not the slightest bit an exaggeration. In foreign countries, however close the friends, it is unusual to invite them to one's house. But in Korea, even without any festive occasion, one is given the privilege of visiting a friend's home under any circumstances. The Westerner's living room is different; but the Korean room is always noisely filled with friends for no special reason. In rural areas there is a custom called "village visiting" in which one goes to a friend's house after dinner as if one had an appointment.

Although Koreans are affectionate and close to their

friends in this way, to strangers they are unexpectedly unfriendly and exclusive. We never greet people whom we don't know well. We don't make any concessions whatsoever to people we don't know. We fight easily. We are shameless. Though someone does us a favor, we don't have the courtesy to reply to him if we don't know him well.

Although we are so polite and affectionate to people we know well, to the general public we are completely cold and discourteous. In meeting strange people, Westerners are more proper than we are, although they inspect each other like dogs who meet and go around and around each other sniffing. When strangers meet on the street, they greet one another with a "good morning." It is also part of their life for strangers to introduce themselves to each other when they sit together drinking in a bar.

When we read Western novels, there are often scenes of strangers talking together of love; but in Korean novels there are almost none. The plots are between friends and the stories are about people who know each other quite well. As proof let's look at the comments of Clifton Fadiman on the novels of Dostoevski. The characters generally meet on the street. They drink a glass of liquor and like intimate friends they open up their inner thoughts and tell stories and confess everything about their lives.

Marshall R. Pihl has made this point. The Korean word "friend" (친구) is a different concept than the word "friend" in English. Its meaning is "close friend," whereas in America when you say "friend" it means only someone you know. In Korea you don't call someone a "friend" if you don't know him well. I guess this has given rise to factionalism.

Also, Father Killoren has said that in any home you are treated warmly when you visit a Korean family. They are polite and friendly. But you get a completely different impression of those you meet on the street. The world of the home and the street are completely separate and so alien. He said quite frankly that unlike the walled world of the family, the world of the street is unfriendly and impolite.

There is no doubt that we are a courteous Oriental country, but this courteousness lies within the wall and amongst people we know. When we go out on the street and when we meet strangers, we change into a people cold blooded and akin to barbarians. Although our morality among friends and family is highly developed, our public morality towards the body of society is dried out.

I suppose that it is absolutely fearful to think that everyone is not a friend. In a bus, in a department store, on the street . . . meeting all those many people there and thinking that they are not one's friends means to be completely cut off from society and individuals. It is a desert scene in which people associate only if they know each other. So, going to a bar or to a park is done in groups. Even if you go to a public place in Korea, you don't find an atmosphere of public togetherness.

25. Two Solitary Islands

ONCE André Maurois characterized England saying, "England does not consist of one island alone, but is rather an archipelago of several million island families." This seems an ordinary comment, but he describes most aptly the traits of the Englishman and English society. Englishmen have an extraordinary respect for the family. But this applies as well to all English-speaking peoples.

Whether they are royalty or commoners, they cherish the inviolability of the independent family. They feel that the family is the basis and the starting point of life. So in their proverbs they compare the home, or family, to a castle and in their folksongs they sing of "Home, Sweet Home." In any situation they try to preserve the rights and the dignity of the family. They cannot conceive of peace, happiness and the joy of life outside of the family. They pay taxes, are patriotic and preserve the rights of the royal household for their own family. So social or national concepts are actually nothing but an extension of the family. The family, the society and the nation do not exist separately, but the family simply becomes the home town, and the home town develops into the nation.

Without long explanations we can grasp this by looking at the English word "home." They call "home" the house in which they live with their parents and their family. They also say "my home town" or "our home country." Moreover, when they refer to a base or a headquarters or a place of origin, they use the word "home."

Baseball is just the same. It is a game in which the player leaves from home plate and returns to home plate. The center of the game is always home plate and the action of the game is the contest to return to that base. Baseball players have various adventures in which their return to home plate is much like Ulysses returning home.

Koreans in their concern for family life do not lag behind the English-speaking peoples. Ours is an extended family system in which even three generations live together. Our sense of the family is as deep as any country in the world.

We like to calculate our genealogical tables and use even our in-laws' distant relatives' names for our own advantage; there are not many other countries which are as completely built on family centrism as is Korea.

But while there have been some changes in recent years, our Korean family has not experienced the real meaning of family life.

Although ours is a family-centered society, the Korean people do not really enjoy living together in the family. All happy events and ceremonies, such as the one hundredth-day ceremony after the birth of a child, are for guests. There are almost no ceremonies in which the family gets together quietly to enjoy each other's company. Usually when there is a party, the members of the household are chased away. There is no time for the family to gather together to chat.

Moreover, in daily life the family members live separately from each other. The father does what he wants and goes out drinking and having a good time with his friends, and the grandfather does what he wants and plays *paduk* under a tree near the pavilion. The only enjoyment the mother has is gossiping with neighborhood wives around the well, and the sister and the elder brother each go their separate ways with their own friends. Also, because there is no one to play with the little children, they play by themselves and are virtually orphans.

But when meal time comes, the family members gather in from here and there as if the home were an inn. If they sit together, the father watches the *nunch'i* of the grandfather and the children watch the *nunch'i* of the father, and there are no words—just the sound of spoons clacking.

The more upper class the household, the more stultifying the atmosphere. It is like a house of the dead. It is thought to be undignified and extraordinary for the family to gather together to have a good time. In England there is no distress like that of a guest entering the family; but in our case we are very glad when he comes in. When a guest joins us, the miasmal family atmosphere comes to life. Talk and games come forth. A natural bridge is made when a third party joins in a family gathering with its strict rank and order of a military camp.

So ours is not a society built family by family, but rather Korean society is constructed by each family member escaping from the family in his own way according to his age and sex.

Of course a wedding invitation is addressed "Mr. and Mrs. so and so invite . . . " but still in our country it is considered awkward and silly for a husband to be accompanied by his wife in public. One may hear this criticized as a foreign custom. So Korean society did not develop like Western European society in terms of its social and national viewpoint as an enlargement of the family—like a ripple in a lake which gradually sketches a broadening circle when a stone is thrown into the water. Society and the family are quite different in Korea.

There is no bridge between society and the family. In this situation often lies the conflict between the family and society, and tragedy results. In Korean society, a "good social being" and a "good family member" are virtually incompatible.

Although Western heroes are also persons who are successful in building a family, in our case it is usually different. The general pattern in Korea is that the hero deserts the family and then becomes a patriot and a public figure. So Korea is not one, but two lonely islands divided into family and society.

Author's note: In Korean society the family does not exist, and in the Korean family, society does not exist. Social life is usually opposite to family life. When we enjoy things it is not like Western Europe where they enjoy family life; instead we have fun with outsiders. Nowadays there are many westernized families. They go on picnics and have a good time together. The main reason families cannot enjoy each other's company lies in our strict family class system. The gap between generations is due to this family system. The elders and the youngsters have no opportunity to associate together. Always, social relations are between the same age groups and the same sex, so generation by generation and sex by sex they build isolated societies which cannot communicate their thoughts to others.

26. Society As Viewed from the Table

Translator's note: A table in Korea is traditionally low and small, often rectangular, rarely rounded. It is used to serve food to one person who is sitting on the floor, although sometimes two to four may use it. The dining table in the Western sense did not exist, and the long low wooden or formica tables used today for parties and in some homes are a relatively modern innovation. Even in families who have long tables, eating is still often done separately.

THERE are no other people like the Koreans for eating solemnly. It is an occasion more solemn and quiet than a funeral ceremony. This is because it is considered a lack of etiquette in our country to talk while eating. We sit quietly and chew away as if we were annoyed. Do we enjoy the taste of food when we have a serious expression as if we were appreciating music?

In comparison, the scene of Westerners eating is too self-indulgent and too noisy. It is impossible to distinguish whether they are eating or rehearsing a speech, or whether they are laughing or babbling. The most merry time of their day seems to be when they are eating.

Moreover, when eating, they flourish in turn a gleaming knife and a fork like spears in a medieval knight's tournament. Although the Last Supper was the occasion when Jesus prophesied his death to his twelve disciples, there must have been less tension than in our meals.

First of all, at the Last Supper they talked; words were bantered to and fro. Although Judas broke the atmosphere, they talked of man's life, and discussed truth and love.

The more we think about it, the more strange it becomes. In all human matters, eating is the most cheerful and lovely event. According to Dr. Menninger, people gathering together to eat is the very first stage of interchanging love. In the life of infants, the first feeling of love and the first expression of affection are communicated through food (the mother's breast) alone. It is not just simple conjecture that the love between mother and child is related to the breast and that human love is exchanged unconsciously through eating. In Christianity, the act of eating is called "communion" and it has a sacred ceremonial meaning; in addition it indicates an "intimate association" and a "spiritual encounter." So food is the road by which one man's heart is opened to another.

If this is so, then looking into our etiquette of eating we may see that the path we trod was unnatural. Actually, the act of eating lays us bare even more than entering a bath.

At the moment of eating, one's face, authority and education are eliminated. The faces of all men are equal when chewing. There is no prince and no slave. Moreover, we cannot even sense the difference between humans and animals.

People reveal themselves more when they associate in a restaurant than they do in a public bath. However great they may be, when they are seated at a table they are nothing but animals with stomachs and teeth. Even when a prima donna has stuffed herself and is sitting completely relaxed picking her teeth, there is no difference between her and an elephant or a hippopotamus in the zoo.

The American army training manual says that enlisted men should not be allowed to look at officers while the latter eat, as the officers would lose their authority. If we think about this in reverse, when people eat together, barriers are lifted and we can say that we enter common ground. But in our Korean case, there was strict stratification and distance between ranks.

In the West the whole family gathers together and eats at one table. While they eat together, they share love. They talk to each other, laugh with and enjoy each other. They communicate with each other as one body around the table. They understand what the elderly are thinking and how the son looks at the world, and what his hobbies and his difficulties are.

We were not this way. The one-third of our whole life which is spent in eating is passed in silence and isolation. We do not have one table; instead a number of tables divide the family. The grandfather's table is different from that of the father. It would be a breach of etiquette for the younger members of the family to be at the same table with their elders. It is impossible to imagine a mother-in-law and a daughter-in-law at the same table. The women are in the kitchen, the grandfather in the guest room, and the children finish eating separated from their parents. If they make noise or play with their spoons while stirring their food, then thunder follows.

Even today in modernized families, it is impossible for all the members of a family to eat together at the same table and enjoy it. First of all, house construction is such that this is impossible. Also, however big the table, it is different from the Western table and more than four people cannot sit at it. I guess this is the reason Koreans have so much stomach trouble.

But in this scene of dining isolation there is one more paradox; the courses on the table are in common. In the West even though people eat together, each person has his own separate portion of food. In our case when we do sit together at one table, except for rice and soup, the other dishes are all eaten from a common bowl. This is another symbol of Korean society.

112

27. "We" and "I"

A certain Japanese scholar was very pessimistic about the word for "I" in Japanese (*watakushi*). The foundation of human life is the subjectivity of "I." So in the language of any country the word "I" is most often used, and therefore as far as the term for the first person singular is concerned, the expression is never difficult or complicated. The syllable is usually simple and the pronunciation easy. The English "I" is so, as is the French *je*, the German *Ich* and the Korean *na*. Only in Japanese is that word, *watakushi*, complicated and long—four syllables long. The most simple and short expression of "I" in Japanese is *boku*, but it is a word which has very restricted use. It must be said this indicates the lack of a subjective concept

113

on the part of the Japanese.

That the Korean for "I" is the monosyllable *na* shouldn't delight us too much. Even though we Koreans have the advantage of an "I" and a distinctive first person subject, curiously enough we use the word *uri,* or "we," more than "I." Like the Japanese scholars who cannot hold their heads high because of their *watakushi,* the Korean scholars feel rather shameful because of the frequent use of "we" instead of "I." On the other hand, there are those who think of this with pride.

To take only one example; when we have to say "my wife," we say "our wife," and with a straight face at that. Foreigners would be very surprised if we were to translate this literally into English. With how many people is that wife living that the husband says "our wife"? Some of our rash friends might jump to conclusions and say that Korean society is polyandrous.

Placing more emphasis on "we" rather than "I" can have a good connotation, depending on the interpretation, for it can be argued that by doing so, more emphasis is always placed upon public consciousness and public destiny rather than on selfish thought. It is better and more modest to say "our house" instead of "my house," and "our country" instead of "my country."

Dictators use a great deal of the first person singular pronoun. In Hitler's and Mussolini's speeches, and, to take an example close to us, in Syngman Rhee's speeches, the word "I" appears with great frequency. In putting "I" ahead of "we," dictatorship sprouts forth.

But the mere fact that we use "we" more than "I" should not affirm that Koreans are that democratic, because "we" without "I" produces despotism. When there is no sense of the individual, and when individual rights are forgotten, the black hands of dictators stretch forth.

The Korean tragedy in large part lies in not finding "I." There is no real "we" because we live without a subject. Korean society is a totality in which "I" is buried within "we." We have lived like a dog on a leash, pulled along by fate or our blood relatives or power. We have not discovered the actual sense of the "I" which determines our independently individual sense.

As I have explained in the chapter "The String Society," our people could not live without depending on something. They could not survive without attaching themselves either to the king or to nature or to family connections.

The officials of the olden days entrusted themselves to the king, and if that was impossible, they surrendered themselves to avoid participation in court and became hermits. So there was just a hairbreadth's difference between the life of the official and the life of the hermit or, to take an analogy from old *sijo* poetry, between "The Song of Loyalty" and "The Song of the White Seagull."[1]

Even the menial laborer in the countryside is more concerned about how others regard him than how he regards himself. From that attitude arises what is called the custom of "outside show" and "face."

It is as Mr. Scofield has said, "Koreans fear more their face being lost than the death of their wife." Because one is fearful of the opinions of others, one becomes a

---

1. "The Song of Loyalty" refers to serving the king loyally in court and "The Song of the White Seagull" refers to hermit life.

chaste widow and a dutiful wife. We worry more about "what others think of me" than "what I think of myself."

Also, we have always lived concealing our self-expression. We value talking about others more than talking about ourselves. It appears in the folksong *Arirang*, "Stars fill the sky and words fill our world." To us "words" means talking ill of others. It is not a dialogue or a discussion which develops between you and me, nor is it the monologue of a confession or a penitence. It is only blaming others. This kind of blame occurs because of our habit of paying too much attention to others' business.

Isn't this like the poem which says "Words make more words so shall we say no more?" We hide ourselves and live according to what others say about us, rather than considering ourselves, so that our individual subjectivity is weakened.

False etiquette, false ornamentation, the attitude of entrusting ourselves to others and being afraid of encountering them, and our liking to criticize others... these occur because of the lack of all sense of individuality and personal recognition. It seems that only at the moment of death do we become conscious of "I." When we are dying we don't say *"Ai-go!* we are dying," but *"Ai-go!* I am dying." If we do not look for the "I" in all situations of desperation, as when we discover the "I" at the moment of death, the real unity of "you" and "me" in "we" will not occur.

28. For Whom Do We Sing?

SINGING is our Korean recreation. In East or West when people gather together to have a good time, whether it is in a bar, a wedding hall or anywhere else, songs naturally come forth. If one is not a singer by profession, a song is supposed to be produced spontaneously. In the West, when everyone gathers together and when they are amused, the whole crowd usually breaks out in song. When this happens the people resemble a chorus of frogs. But our Korean case is not like this; strangely enough, the crowd always asks an individual to sing.

117

Asking someone else to sing a song has become a kind of etiquette when we are relaxing. To sing without being asked is a breach of good taste. The method and the procedure of asking someone to sing are not so simple. First, the person who is to sing is indicated by democratic procedure. Each of the singers is chosen one by one by the opinion of the crowd. But even when the singer is chosen, it does not mean he will sing without hesitation. Even at such times we make a virtue of politely declining.

If everyone repeatedly asks someone to sing, he must object strongly. After escaping many times, he finally gives in and sings a melody in a clear voice.

The strange thing is, when the performance finally begins, the very people who had asked the singer to sing are the ones who don't listen enthusiastically. They ask someone to sing and when he does they turn to their neighbors and offer them cups of wine which are declined; this goes on in a kind of partial but friendly conflict. When the song seems about over, then everyone becomes interested in the singer and they applaud and ask for an encore.

The point is that we seem more interested in asking someone to sing than in the song itself. (In the West they have drinking songs but in Korea we have a song asking someone to drink.) Also, it is not that the singer delays singing because he doesn't want to. The proof is that if he declines once and the finger is pointed at someone else to sing or if no one asks him to sing, then he feels that the party was depressing and spoiled. He feels bad and returns home lonely with a blank expression and an unsatisfied appearance.

So for whom do we sing? It is not because we are

forced to sing nor do we want to sing.

Singing is an emotion. So asking someone to sing is like forcing an emotion. And to sing by invitation means producing an unnatural emotion. You cannot understand Koreans without knowing about the emotion of singing not by others' will nor by one's own will.

If you are a foreigner, you can never accept at face value Koreans saying "no," or for that matter, their saying "yes." No matter how pleased they are, they must decline several times first, so you must repeat the invitation several times. You ask, expecting to be refused, and one refuses, expecting to be asked again; such is the "theory of relativity" which even Dr. Einstein did not discover so early.

Korean human relations are based upon this "theory of relativity" of asking and declining, and if you do not act in accordance with the circumstances, you will make many mistakes.

It is different from a cocktail party. That scene is one in which you take a glass, go and pour your own drink and eat the hors d'oeuvres you have selected. It is a party in which there is no one to ask you to drink and no one to decline; in Korean eyes it is tasteless and uninteresting. Moreover, although the core of the cocktail party is talking, in Korea too much talking is considered to be a breach of etiquette. To us it means boasting or a loss of the sense of self-possession.

This is true not only in singing, but in daily life as well. In inviting and declining, we share the warm emotion of relations with others. Im Paek-ho is said to have sung this song at the grave of the *kisaeng* Hwang Chin-i

119

(although some doubt that he actually did so): "There is no one to offer me drink, so I am sad." The people of our country, whoever they may be, think that not to be asked is something very regretful. Surely our method of social intercourse, in which we like something and pretend it is bad or if it is bad we pretend we like it, has different implications than the method of the Westerner who dissects and analyzes everything.

But on the other hand, because of this system of dual social relations in which one is not frank, misunderstandings are produced if one does not fit the situation. It is like people who meet on a cloudy day or in the mist and haze. Although the vague images have a mysterious sentiment, if one is mistaken, there is danger of a clash.

In such a situation songs flow forth, in chorus and solo . . . not in one's own joy nor for others', such vague songs. . . .

These strange songs still come from the corners of Korean society. The words we often use nowadays, "half voluntarily and half by another's will" may have come from this. We don't say "no," and we don't say "yes"; instead we live with each other by hinting even before we speak.

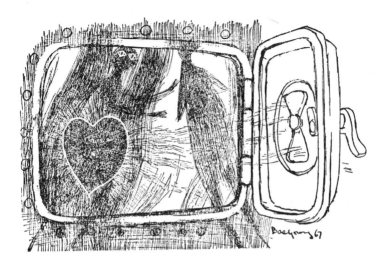

29. On Love

IF Westerners' love can be compared to a stove, we can use the metaphor of a brazier or *ondol* heating to describe Koreans' love. In the main, Westerners' love resembles both the heat and the coldness of a stove which, after burning furiously, leaves a heap of ashes. Love comes on so very quickly, like an epidemic of the plague. Westerners think that there is a profound relationship between love and death. Their love is always paired with death. It is like a red-hot stove and a cold stove. Love starts with flames and love expires with flames.

But we can say that rather than ardently burning, Koreans' love begins to smoulder after it has burnt out. It is like the embers buried in the ashes of a brazier or the warmth in an *ondol* floor. In the pleasant heat of an *ondol*

121

room and in a warm brazier which has no flames, there is an earthy warmth like restrained passion and a life-giving reverberation towards eternity.

When we stir the ashes in a cooled brazier on a winter night, we can still see some embers remaining. And this remaining warmth underneath the *ondol* floor reminds us of the human temperature. The love of the Korean is subtle, like the embers buried in the ashes and the deeply buried warmth under the *ondol* floor.

Our word for love in our old language originally meant "to think." Thinking was love, and love thinking. So the emotion of affection, which seeps forth like a spring, matches the nature of the Korean more than the violent and openly active love of the Westerner. The way of this love, which is neither easily warmed nor easily cooled, is, in a strict sense, "affection" more than "love."

When Westerners love, without exception they confess "I love you" or *Je t'aime*. But Koreans, even if they are westernized, don't directly spit out the word "love." In Chŏng Ch'ŏl's[1] famous poem "Thinking of a Beautiful Person," we find such an exclamation as "There seems to be a subtle change in your manner as you greeted me." As indicated in this quotation, love and hate are emotions subtly shown by expressions on the face; they are not stated. With such an expression love is confessed, or with a slight change of expression the grief of a cooled affection is felt. This is different in degree of tragedy from a love which is like sparks flying and iron melting in a blast furnace.

Although Werther liquidated his grief over lost love

1. One of the most famous of Yi Dynasty poets, 1537-1594

122

with a pistol, a Korean Werther doesn't use a pistol, but tosses and turns, sleepless on his pillow.

All the old songs of parting are like this. In Chŏng Ch'ŏl's "*Kasiri*" (가시리) or in the "Ode on Leaving the Western Capital" (西京別曲), departing lovers are sent off quietly, as in the poem:

> *If I try and stop you, you will be hurt,*
> *And so I let you go*
> *Hoping in vain you will someday return.*

Though she knows that her lover crosses the river to meet another woman, her song of farewell is one in which she unreasonably blames the guiltless boatman who has taken him away. Resigned, she doesn't even touch her lover's sleeve nor blame him, though he has abandoned her.

Isn't the song *Arirang* just like this? The Korean love drama is not the same as the story "Carmen," where the betraying lover is stabbed with a dagger. Either the Korean maidens sit helplessly waiting for their departing lovers to get footsore and return to them after travelling only ten *li*, or they act like the disappointed girl the poet So-wŏl described who scattered azalea petals in the path of her departing lover to hide her emotion.[2]

---

2. Kim So-wŏl (1903–1934). The reference is to the poem "The Azalea"(from *Anthology of Korean Poetry*, Lee):

You're sick and tired of me.
When you go
I'll bid you goodbye without saying
  a word.

I'll gather azaleas on Yak Mountain,
The burning azaleas of Yŏngbyŏn
And strew them in your path.

Tread gently, please,
Step by step, softly,
On the flowers of dedication.

You're sick and tired of me.
When you leave
I'll not weep though I die.

It is not because we Koreans are so greatly generous, but because our women have tried to contain the reflections of their love in their forbearance and meek obedience. It may be a deeper grief to say, "When you leave, I'll not weep though I die" than the sorrowful heart which cries out loud. Resignation, self-control and forbearance —the heart which has lost love is more yearning. Like the embers buried in the ashes, it is an emotion which is not easily extinguished.

More than people of other countries, Koreans long for and hunger after love. Others have said this and we also have felt it. But while we love, our love is rather tepid compared with other peoples'.

Naturally, what is called "love" is too often for us a love of departing rather than a love of meeting. It is a love made up of the weariness of waiting and the exhaustion of seeing others off. That is why there are pairs of mandarin ducks[3] and pairs of flying butterflys pictured on screens or on the sides of Korean pillows; the only wish and the only happiness is to take an oath that at least the souls will be together.

So rather than progressing, Koreans' love is in large part in the past tense.

We are a people who cherish our love in our memories after the fire of love has gone out, like melting ourselves on the warmed *ondol* floor or picking out the burnt embers buried in the ashes of the brazier. This love is like

---

3. Mandarin ducks, because of their proverbial faithfulness, are a common symbol of conjugal happiness in Far Eastern art, and they are often found in the decoration of the homes of the newly married.

a young widow. It is a memory of love. I guess this gave rise to the custom of life-long celibacy for the widow after the husband or lover was lost.

In the West, if the lover disappears, love is finished. But in our case we can say that after the lover disappears, love begins. Korean love is affection *in absentia*.

30. Song of the Long, Long Night

IT was not a love under the glaring sun of the Mediterranean nor one at burning noon in the lands of the sun-worshipers. Korean romances are murmurs in the dim night under the chilly moonlight.

It all happened on such a night: The poetess and *kisaeng* Hwang Chin-i took the reins of Pyŏk Ke-su's horse and Ch'unhyang dried her tears in prison. Korean love songs are all about the long night; they are not for the mid-day, but for the long night and the depiction of the emotion of night.

> *Were I to build a bamboo hut on the ice,*
> *Were I to die of cold with him on the ice,*
> *O night, run slow, till our love is spent.*[1]

The women of the Koryŏ Dynasty sang this kind of song. To sing about love was simply a hymn to night,

---

1. *Anthology of Korean Poetry*, Lee.

and to pray for love meant wishing for night to stretch out indefinitely.

Hwang Chin-i's *sijo* poem is just the same:

> *I cut in two*
> *A long November night, and*
> *Place half under the coverlet,*
> *Sweet-scented as a spring breeze,*
> *And when he comes, I shall take it out,*
> *Unroll it inch by inch, to stretch the night.*[2]

Even though there is a distinct difference between these two poems, there is no difference in the hope and wish that morning would come slowly and night would remain. In any country love between the sexes is made at night. Koreans are not alone in trying to keep the mystery and happiness of night for even a moment longer. The Koreans' nights were, however, felt to be shorter and more evanescent than elsewhere. This was because in Korea the relations between the sexes were not free and were hampered by severe restrictions. As the term *kyujung kwŏllyŏ* (閨中궐녀 segregation of women in wealthy homes) indicates, the young were imprisoned in the recesses of the family. In this kind of society illegitimate love affairs had to exist and were turned into dreams of youth, lonely and full of sighs buried in the heart. Their love shared the fate of the moon which only shines at night. Only at night are they free for a moment from the eyes of others and from moral chains.

> *There is so much talk about the daughter-in-law of*
> *other families,*

---

2. *Ibid.*

They cannot play with their husbands by day.
So let's play at night, hai-di-ho.

An analysis of this kind of folksong reveals the relationship between night and love. Love was like robbery; it had to be done at night.

Contrarily, in the West, gods of Mount Olympus made love under the bright sky. The love of the Greeks took place in broad daylight. And how about the love of Zeus? What about the love of the gods who teased the nymphs by throwing stones at them and flirting while they were bathing in the valley full of jade-like water?

That love was one exuberantly joyful of life itself rather than sinful, one which celebrates the beauty of body itself. Unlike our love, wrapped in a curtain of night, theirs took place under the blessing of light, a banquet of Eros.

Because we have lived under such a custom of love, we have been poorly trained not only in the relations between the sexes but in love for humanity. Therefore, in old novels and stories, we read more stories about love for unreal objects than stories concerned with love for living persons. In the *Kŭmosinhwa* (金鰲神話 "New Stories of the Golden Turtle")[3] is a story about a youth named Yangseng who is in love with a ghost. The "Cloud Dream of the Nine" (九雲夢)[4] is a love story with eight fairies. In rural guestrooms the majority of the old stories which are bantered back and forth are the stories of brides who have been changed into women from snails, centipedes, snakes or foxes. It is love for the image of a girl who is unreal and

3. By Kim Si-sŭp (1435–1493)
4. By Kim Man-jung (1637–1692)

128

who disappears like an illusion at cockcrow.

Even love with a girl in reality was the same; young unmarried boys and girls had no love. If there were romances, they were with *kisaeng*, called "night girls," or female slaves or widows.

If Ch'unhyang had not been the daughter of an old *kisaeng*, but the daughter of a *yangban*, there would have been no story. This is how stories like Ch'unhyang were produced.

Great or small, night love is an unhealthy one. It is a sorrowful and empty love. At daybreak it disappears like the waning moon. Many have lived their lives without knowing what love is. A society in which love between the sexes was not possible was one which longed for the night, wrapped in dim moonlight rather than active sunlight. In such a society, one's self cannot shine brightly but lives like the moon in the reflection of others.

Author's note: The names of Korea, *asadal* (아사달) or later Chosŏn, are related to a primitive religion worshiping the sun, not the night or the moon. But from the time of our suffering, we have liked darkness more than clearness and the lonely moon more than the sun.

Among Korean stories, the favorite is about the wife who came from a snail. When an old bachelor lamented his fate while he tilled the field saying "With whom may I live?" there was a sound "Live with me." He thought it strange and looked around to see the point from which the sound came. There was a snail. He picked it up and took it home. Later, a beautiful girl appeared from the snail and prepared dinner for him. So they lived together. Most of the old stories begin this way; later the woman disappeared.

31. Moonlight Customs

IN the West there are many folksongs praising the sun. Among them "O Sole Mio" is perhaps typical. When Westerners talk about their lovers or about life, they naturally refer to them as "my sun."

But in our country, in our *sijo* poetry and folksongs, we find little of the sun. All of our songs are about the moon. We are a people who surely like the dim moon more than the fiercely burning bright sun. There has been no distinction by age or sex in our songs of love to the moon. The elderly play the *kŏmunko* and tip their winecups while looking at the moon which is sitting on the bent bow of an old pine tree.

Don't take out the straw mat.
Why can't we sit on the fallen leaves?
Don't light the pine resin lamp,
The moon which set last night will rise again.
Boy! don't say there isn't any lousy wine or wild
*   vegetables.*
Just bring them along.

However poor one's life, just looking at the moon is enough to make one feel like an immortal.

Children, their eyes opened wide with wonder, look at the round moon as children will. In their dreams they sing about the cinnamon tree and the rabbit in the moon, and they see the sliver of the moon as a tiny boat crossing the silver river of the Milky Way. In their song, their homely desire is to live forever on the moon with their parents in a small thatched hut built from the cinnamon tree. The point is that the children's song reflects their hearts and is too restricted and too lonely a desire. But because the children grow up seeing reality as troublesome, they love the eternal moon more than their rough land. At most, their poor dream is not for a great, high, tiled house, but for a thatched house, as small as possible.

In accordance with the waxing and the waning of the moon's shadow, we have marked our time and our festivals. The Westerners use the solar calendar to determine their festivals and this creates quite an opposite atmosphere.

So among the Korean festivals, the most important is *Ch'usŏk* which occurs just at the full moon of the eighth lunar month. We are a people who are happy if we only can eat and have a beautiful bright moon, as in our saying

"Not more and not less than the August moon of *Ch' usŏk*."

In olden days the festival of *Ch' usŏk* at the time of the full moon of August (which falls in September by the solar calendar) was the best festival the people had. Men would wrestle or play the game of turtle and enjoy youth. And for the women who stayed indoors throughout the year, this was the only time they could go outside and sing and dance to their hearts' desire.

Under the light of the round, really round, moon they had no shyness or restraint. In groups of twenty or thirty they would hold hands and dance around in a circle representing the full moon. Perhaps then for the first time they would feel the enjoyment of living. For the first time they would feel youth and perhaps love.

Moreover, on that day the boys and girls would mingle together and play at tug-of-war; the moon was just about the only thing that could cause the miracle of bringing the sexes together. Besides *Ch' usŏk*, the full moon of January did the same thing.

The custom of *Tapkyŏ*, crossing the bridge at the full moon of January, was more romantic to the young than the games of *Ch' usŏk*. From the time of King Chung Jong (reigned 1506–1544) of the Yi Dynasty, there was, on the full moon of January, the custom of crossing a bridge as many times as one's age. Although one was supposed to do this to escape from the disasters of a whole new year, I guess the main objective actually was to play together at the time of the full moon. It was a poetic custom for the boys and girls to gather together and promenade on the bridge under the chilly winter moonlight. How much they loved the moon is evident, for they could not lightly dismiss the cold moon trembling in the bitter wind. It is written in the *P'aegwan chapki* (稗官雜記)[1] that crossing the bridge was considered to be crossing the bridge of love.

The boys teased the girls and gathered together to follow them around, flirting and secretly holding their hands. Like the legend of the shepherd and the shepherdess, who live in the sky and meet once a year when they cross the Milky Way bridge on the seventh day of the seventh month, the boys and girls could only meet the opposite sex on this one day, which was for them their bridge.

There is a moon and there is a lover; thus this is the happiest night. The atmosphere is quite different from that of a Western carnival.

In this way, the moon brought life, joy and happiness. But moonlight was not simply beautiful and joyous. They say that Admiral Yi Sun-sin invented the custom of *Kang Kang Suwŏllae,* or dancing in a circle holding hands, in order to unify the people and control their emotions during the Japanese invasion of 1592. So, how many tears and sighs are there behind this sort of playing in the moonlight? When we hear the melody that's sung while dancing, our hearts are moved by the sorrowful tune. Moreover, if we analyze the lyrics of that song, we are even more amazed.

The content of the song which begins "The candle, the candle, the jade candle..." is an appeal to expatiate the death of a girl. This girl, who lived with her in-laws, had to sew by lamp light. No one cared enough to tell her to put out the lamp and sleep; but the wind blew between

1. Ŏ Suk-kwŏn, *Miscellaneous Notes of a Storyteller,* (fl. 1554)

the rice-paper doors, extinguishing the light, and the exhausted woman fell asleep. At that moment the husband returned. The mother-in-law told her son that his wife slept all the time and, as an excuse, said the wind blew out the light. The story ends with the wife taking a silver knife and stabbing herself to death. Why is there such brutality and the smell of blood in this song that they sing in the beautiful silent moonlight? In this way the moon is not only a sign of happiness but also a symbol of lament.

The waxing and waning moon dies and is reborn again. The moonlight which appears and disappears countless times in the dark is the shadow of despair and hope and life and death.

The new moon promises a full moon and in the ruin of the waning moon is the promise of a new moon. It is neither dark nor light. The song of the girls dancing is a paradoxical mixture of both joy and tears. It seems that our love of the indistinct moonlight is from a great deal of sadness and lament in our life.

32. Women

THE following story appeared in an anthology of American humor. Once an American visited Korea before the Korean War and saw a scene on a mountain path in which a man was riding a donkey and his wife followed behind, panting. The American was startled and asked, "Hey, don't you know the proper way of treating women? Ladies first! Don't treat women so badly." Expressionless, the Korean gentleman answered, "This is our custom."

However, when the American again visited Korea just after the Korean War, he saw quite an opposite picture. This time, on the same mountain path, the woman was riding a donkey in front and the man carefully followed far behind. The American thought this curious. He said, "Hey, your customs have changed from before, haven't they?" But the gentleman replied without batting an eye, "I'm sorry. Since the war my wife goes in front because there are landmines buried all around here."

This humor dramatized the Korean custom of complete male superiority and female subordination. Americans may scorn our male superiority, but we can't stop laughing at their society in which the female is superior and the male inferior.

When we look at Western movies, we often see scenes in which a woman slaps the cheek of an upstanding man. If a gentleman hits a lady, that is considered barbarous; but if a lady hits a gentleman, then it seems that they think this is cultured.

In our eyes, we cannot understand the Western male who, though slapped on the cheek by a woman, still seems to enjoy it. The degree of development of Western civilization is directly proportional to the increased rate of henpecked husbands. It seems strange to us that the most prominent Western intellectual, Socrates, is the prime example of the henpecked husband. But it is very doubtful whether Westerners follow the principle of "ladies first" when entering an air-raid shelter to escape from bombing.

If we think about it, the doctrine of "ladies first" is nothing but luxurious male exaggeration, although they may think of it as the virtue of protecting the weak. To me it is really a somewhat abnormal masochistic psychology.

It is just the same as their habit of elevating women by making nude statues of them or calling them the "goddess of luck."

Male and female superiority are both unnatural, but we must mention the point that the Korean woman spends

136

her whole life in the unhappy position of obedience. The history of the Korean, or Oriental, woman is a history of obedience and humiliation.

This is obvious if we look at what is called the Confucian "Way of the Three Female Obediences" and the "Seven Reasons for Expelling a Wife." The former says, "When young, a woman is obedient to her parents; when married, to her husband; and when old, to her son." And the latter indicates that when a woman marries, the husband need not hesitate in expelling her and sending her back to her parents if she does not serve her parents-in-law well, if she has no children, if she is lecherous, too jealous, has an incurable disease, or if she talks too much or steals.

This custom is quite different from that of Rome, where there was a "code for judging love" which contained thirty-one articles. It said, "It is unreasonable for marriage to exclude love"; and it recommended that "real jealousy heightens the price of love" rather than being one of the seven reasons for expelling a wife, as it is in our society.

They have written in their code, which is a "code of love," that they recognize the woman's "right to love." Moreover, there is one line in it that says if a husband dies after two years the wife may remarry.

But to the Korean woman, the Confucian virtues of etiquette and morality have always been more important than love. It is more honest to say that a woman marries a commandant rather than a man. So women generally must spend their lives in love's broken hopes, in regret and tears.

If we examine the folksongs of the inner court where the women reside, we will find that they lament the plight of widows, concubines, the difficulty of living together with one's in-laws, and farewells.

> *My mother shouldn't have borne me*
> *She should have borne a pear which she could have sold.*
> *My father shouldn't have given me life*
> *He should've made a mat seat instead of lying on the mat with her.*
> *Why did they give me life that I must bear this hardship?*

The women of this land have lived their lives and then died resenting and regretting having been born. Women's existence isn't recognized even as much as that of a mat.

Moreover, born in a weak country, the Korean woman has borne two great catastrophes.

> *You harvest barley when it's ripe;*
> *How can you pick a maiden when she isn't ripe yet?*
> *Even the butterfly knows where to sit*
> *But they break the branch before the flower blooms.*

During the reign of King T'aechong, when Chinese emissaries came and selected beautiful Korean girls for presentation to the Chinese court, they took the very young ones who were not even adults. That is why this song was sung. They were chased and broken before they could fully bloom.

Quite opposite to Pascal who said that if Cleopatra's nose had been slightly longer, the history of the world would have changed—if the nose of the Korean woman were longer, Korean history would be about the same.

138

The Korean tragedy is one degree darker because of our treatment of our women.

Author s note: We have a proverb which says that if you don't beat a woman for three days, she will become a fox and run away to the mountain. This comes from the view that women must be restrained and suppressed. Women look down on themselves rather than men being contemptuous of them. Another proverb commonly used among women is "When the hen cries, the home will be destroyed." To be beautiful is woman's highest ideal, but in our country being beauti ul was a disgrace and often the root of disaster. Even if we do not pay attention to the proverb "Beautiful women die young," when a woman was beautiful, she had a bad life or had no recourse other than to become a *kisaeng.* Beautiful women were suspected of being crafty.

Baeyoung 67

33. Living with In-laws

Translator's note: In Korean there are different terms for living with one's husband's family (시집살이) and living with one's wife's family (처가살이). Unless otherwise indicated, the term "in-law" is used here to mean living with the husband's family.

WHY did we Koreans use the terms "going to live with one's wife's parents" or "going to one's husband's parent's home" for marriage? We do not have a native Korean word for marriage, as have the Chinese (結婚). If we investigate these terms, perhaps they can explain quite easily the Korean concept of marriage.

In English the term "to wed" basically means a promise or an oath. It appears that they think of marriage as a promise between the sexes, like a contract for merchandise.

But we do not think of marriage as a contract. The term *sichip* (시집) does not mean the husband; rather, it means the husband's house. So *sichip kanda* (시집간다) is not going to live with a man, but literally it means going to live with that family, the husband's parents. It is the same with the term for living together with one's wife's parents in their house, *changga* (장가); it is done as a unit.

In our old customs, which are the same as those of the Koguryŏ Kingdom, when a man wanted to get a wife, he had to live with his wife's parents and look after the household until after the birth of his first son, and then he would take his wife to their own home.

So Korean marriage is not a union of a man with one woman, but is considered to be a plural union of oneself with a family. In Korea there was no consciousness of the individual, and the individual personality was not recognized; only the family was considered.

The husband himself exists only as a part of the family. So naturally there is no independent relationship between the husband and the wife in marriage; however, she has to be particularly considerate of her relationships with the whole family. Here begins the abnormal married life of living with one's in-laws.

Among our folksongs and folktales, the greatest portion are related to the sadness of living with one's in-laws. Living with one's in-laws means married life and at the same time a life of restraint.

The proverb "Deaf three years and dumb three more

years" makes just this point. The daughter-in-law must pretend to be deaf for three years and dumb for three more years in order to live with her husband's family.

> *Living with in-laws is a dog's life.*
> *No matter how hot pepper is*
> *Living with in-laws is hotter still.*

We can deduce how much suffering and restraint of freedom there is in this kind of life by looking at folk-songs of this type. All family relationships begin and end in restraint and conflict.

> *Although it is difficult to pass another person on a*
> *single-track bridge,*
> *My husband's father is more difficult.*
> *Although the tree's leaf is green,*
> *Greener with anger and envy is my mother-in-law's*
> *face.*
> *My husband's brother's wife is like a bird who gives*
> *me dirty looks,*
> *My husband's sister is a bird who always complains,*
> *My husband's father is a pompous bird,*
> *And my husband,*
> *He is plain foolish.*

In this way human relationships are mixed with discontent and oppression. In such a void, love with one's husband cannot go smoothly.

By the time the wife has just begun to monopolize her husband, when they are old and her in-laws have died, then "the wife's face, which had been as pretty as the flower of the bindweed, has become as ugly as a pumpkin flower; and her hair, which had been as fine as hemp, has become as rough as the bark of the bushclover; and her hands, which had been like white jade, have become as wrinkled as duck's feet." Then the beautiful clothes of her youth are gone, "rotted from the wiping of tears."

Then usually the husband takes a concubine. Here the vicious circle is repeated. Originally, living with in-laws is obeying the husband's mother's orders. The relationship between the mother-in-law and the daughter-in-law is always the relationship of antagonists.

We can explain the reason for this by reversing Freud's Oedipus complex. First, the reason the mother-in-law hates her daughter-in-law is that the mother can no longer monopolize her son's love. Also the mother-in-law in her youth had to live with her in-laws, too.

Because of living with her in-laws, her love with her husband has become severed. Naturally there is no other object on which the mother-in-law can pour her affection, so her compensation is to transfer her severed love for her husband to her son and to sublimate all her pain and loneliness through this channel.

In any country this is so, but the Korean mother-in-law, especially, loves her son because her married life has been unhappy. This is close to drowning in blind love. When a new competitor, the daughter-in-law, appears, we can imagine how fierce the mother-in-law's envy and struggle is. So the ill treatment of the daughter-in-law begins. This is living with one's in-laws.

The daughter-in-law once again walks the same path her mother-in-law walked. So when the daughter-in-law becomes a mother-in-law, exactly the same situation of living with one's in-laws occurs. A proverb says just this: "When the daughter-in-law who has been badly treated becomes a mother-in-law, she treats her daughter-in-law even worse." The failure of marital relations brings again the vicious circle of life with in-laws and in that vicious circle is repeated the conflict, jealousy and confusion of the Korean family. If we enlarge this problem, it simply becomes Korean society and Korean history.

In the West, it is the relationship between the daughter's mother and her son-in-law which is bad, not that between the husband's mother and the daughter-in-law.

In one of their cartoons, a boxer is practicing punching a sandbag and the coach says, "Hit it again. Think of the sandbag as your mother-in-law's face." This is because the wife's mother tries to interfere with the couple's independent married life. Because they try to keep their own independent life, the wife's mother's presence creates disharmony; and in our case, because the mother-in-law tries to absorb completely another person into her hands, we may say that disharmony is created between the husband's mother and his wife. These two situations are quite a contrast.

If we enlarge this kind of relationship, we can define for ourselves the character of Western and Oriental society. Isn't the vicious circle of living with one's in-laws like our present political struggles between the government party and the opposition?

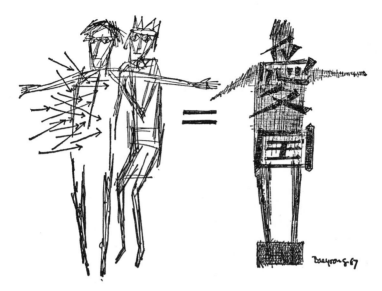

34. On Patriotism

Translator's note: This article was written shortly after the Student Revolution. The author has indicated that some of his views have been modified since then.

KOREAN history is one in which there has been a great deal of hardship from foreign aggression. This type of history has given birth to Koreans who maintain a violent hatred of foreign enemies. Although rulers sometimes compromised or surrendered, among the people there arose the tradition that they had never surrendered.

"The heroes who fended off the invasions of foreign enemies have become myths to the people and their exploits have been continuously handed down by the farmers. However fanciful the contents of these legends may be, they are believed and enjoyed. In them we can glimpse the traditions of a people who have grown up in suffering."

This quotation is from the conclusion of a history of Korea written by a Japanese, Mr. Hatada, who stood in the forefront of the "Movement To Save Lee Chin-u's Life." As that historian said, even today we do not forget the names of our people's heroes and patriots.

However ignorant the farmer or however young the child, they each know the stories of Admiral Lee Sun-sin who defeated the Japanese in the Imjin War of 1592, and of the *kisaeng* Nonkae who threw herself and a Japanese general over a cliff into the river in 1593, and of Saimdang, a famous scholar, and of the three thousand court ladies of Paekche who threw themselves over a cliff as a protest against the Silla conquest.

However few they may be, all the statues in our land are of people who fought and died for the country. This tradition of statues and tablets continues today. Examples are the tablets to those loyal spirits who were killed in the Korean War or in the Student Revolution of April 19, 1960.

This is quite different from the situation in the West. The English love the birthplace of Shakespeare more than they love the statue of Nelson. In Germany they revere the statues of Goethe and Shiller and the death mask of Beethoven. One need not mention the statues or monuments in the center of Paris or even those scattered everywhere in the city and the Louvre Museum.

Our spirit has been ruled by political patriots and heroes, while the Western tradition has been ruled by cul-

146

tural heroes, those who created culture and the arts.

The English used to say that they would rather give up India than lose Shakespeare. But to us this metaphor does not exist. We would have given up a writer of ours, although he was as great as Shakespeare, but we would not have wanted to lose India.

But this is not because we do not love art or culture. It is because in our history we have had no spare time for it. The reality of our history has been that rather than write one line of poetry, we have tried to keep one span of our land, and rather than compose one song, we have tried to live without disaster for one day. So if our poems do not express our own personal emotions, they are odes to our rulers. However beautiful our lyric poems may be, if we examine them carefully, they are just like martial songs. The "lover" who appears in poetry and song is not the usual lover, but the king or the country. Common love songs were sung by cheap *kisaeng*.

This patriotic lament of Chŏng Mong-ju (1337–92), who was killed by the first Yi Dynasty king because he was faithful to the Koryŏ king, has been believed intensely and fervently:

> *Were I to die a hundred times,*
> *Then die and die again,*
> *And all my bones no more than dust,*
> *My soul gone far from men,*
> *Yet still my red blood, shed for you,*
> *Shall witness that my heart was true.*[1]

We have existed more by praising the dead than by

---

1. *Anthology of Korean Poetry*, Lee.

147

praising the living. We consider the famous "Six Dead Officials"[2] to be more glorious than the "Six Live Officials."

To put it in a rather extreme way, we have a prejudice that the living are all criminals and that the dead are heroes. If Lee Chun had not died in the Hague where he had gone to plead for Korean independence in 1919, and had instead lived to return to Korea, no one would have remembered his name. Miss Yu Kwan-sun, who was killed by the Japanese in the March 1, 1919 Independence Movement, and the loyal official Min Ch'ung-chŏng, who killed himself in protest against the Japanese protectorate over Korea in 1905, are just the same.

The patriotism of the Koreans is one which is written in blood. It is a patriotism like that of the woman who became a model wife by biting her finger and giving her blood to her parents. Ours is a situation in which we feel we cannot love our country without shedding our own blood. We do not think it especially patriotic to pay our taxes or do our duty or preserve the natural resources of our land. There are many of our people who think that it is not patriotic to stir flasks in a laboratory or to study in some classroom, although they feel that carrying placards and going out into the street to demonstrate is.

It is a patriotism of self-destruction for the public

---

2. "The Six Dead Officials": They were Sŏng Sam-mun (성삼문), Pak P'aeng-nyŏn (박팽년), Ha Wi-chi (하위지), Yi Kae (이개), Yu Eung-pu (유응부) and Yu Sŏng-wŏn (유성원). They were killed in 1456 by King Sejo, who was the 7th king of the Yi Dynasty, because they tried to restore the former King Tanjong who had been driven away. They are regarded as paragons of the faithful retainer.

148

good where the word "desperateness" is the slogan. It is not a quiet patriotism, but a noisy one, and not a creative patriotism, but a defensive one. It seems as if it is impossible for the self and the state to coexist peacefully. Patriotism starts with the sacrifice of the self and the denial of one's happiness. It is a patriotism in which one must foam at the mouth and have bloodshot eyes. In Korea, to be both patriotic and alive is difficult.

Myths are just the same. The epic poetry of Greece and Rome expresses their thoughts on concepts of death, love and human destiny. But our myths generally are not concerned with human life but are rather about our leaders and the founders of the nation. They are myths about politics and rulers.

Our modern myths are the same, and this is evident if we read our newspapers which have made them. The newspapers in our country emphasize politics and politicians. Not many other countries give such importance to the political aspects of life as do the makers of our newspapers. While a few words uttered in a hotel room by some spokesman for the many small political parties appear in headlines as big as a fist, a dissertation written over some tens of years spent in obscure research study receives only two or three lines in the newspaper's cultural column. It is sound to say that the tradition of our history has been built on political consciousness and resistance. But the facts of our situation are that we lack concern for the basic life of human beings and the creative power of a peaceful life. While praising the blood-stained skirt of Yu Kwan-sun, we have forgotten the gentle touch of Hwang Chin-i playing the *kŏmunko*.

So our patriotism is not the face of tens of thousands of patriots like Yu Kwan-sun, but the features of a single person standing alone as in the poem of Sŏng Sam-mun (1418–1456):

> *Were you to ask me what I'd wish to be*
> *In the world beyond this world,*
> *I could answer, a pine tree, tall and hardy*
> *On the highest peak of Mt. Pongnae,*
> *And to be green, alone green,*
> *When snow fills heaven and earth.*[3]

Author's note: Of course our country is a nation of scholars. Our "culture-first" policy brought about our love of letters and we ignored military affairs. But why do we say our country is not cultured? Truly this is a paradox. The reason is that the scholar was not independent and always had a political tie, so the arts were always interwoven with politics. As religion overpowered culture in Europe during the Middle Ages, our culture, which was not separate from politics, did not have its own domain. Everything in the field of culture has been officially controlled.

Let me introduce one of my previous columns. The air which we breath in Vienna is musical, and even the silence sings. Once Jean Cocteau said that Vienna is the city of music. It is not an exaggeration to say that in my experience, wherever you go in Vienna you can find concerts and music programs. And even the names of the stores and even the streets are named after famous musicians. So naturally even the air seems musical. Not only that, but memorial statues of musicians stand in every part of the city.

---

3. *Anthology of Korean Poetry*, Lee.

150

But Korea is different from Vienna. The air which we breath in Seoul is the air of demonstrations. We could say that even the silence demonstrates. In Seoul there are many famous places connected with demonstrations. First, there is the March 1, 1919 demonstration area of Pagoda Park which was the center of the demonstrations against the Japanese. City Hall plaza was the center of the April 19, 1960 student uprising, as was Taepyŏngno and the entrance to the presidential mansion, etc. These places are remembered as monuments to history. On our campuses there stand student memorial statues to those who fell while demonstrating, not statues of musicians. This is a symbol of political tragedy and hurts us. How do foreigners feel when they see the statues of musicians in Vienna? What if they were to come to Korea and see the memorial statues of those who sacrificed their lives while demonstrating? There can not be aesthetics and peace in Seoul, as there is in Vienna, without political and economic security.

Baeyoong 67

35. Korean and Western Playing Cards

Translator's note: Korean cards are called *hwat'u* (花鬪 lit. battle of flowers) as most of them have pictures of flowers. There are forty-eight cards in the deck, eleven sets of four each for eleven months of the year and a set of four symbolizing rain. In referring to Western cards, Koreans use the term "trump" for the Western deck in general, a misuse of the bridge term applied to all card games played with Western cards.

IT was during my primary school days. One day our pockets were inspected and they found several playing cards, Korean and Western. As I had no excuse for having them, I was punished. Of course, I had not the slightest intention of playing with either the Western or the Korean cards.

First, I didn't have a whole set. I had gleaned a few cards from the trash can in my elder brother's study and from the fire hole for the *ondol* in the guestroom. Finding the pictures interesting, I put the cards in my pocket and occasionally took them out and admired them secretly, as I would cartoons or pictures of children's games.

While I was kneeling in an empty classroom as punishment, the pictures on the Korean and Western cards flashed before my eyes, wet with tears. The arrogant king wearing his crown stared at me, his moustache like the Chinese character for eight (八). When the lonely shadow of the full moon on the Korean card disappeared, somewhere a frog jumped up to a willow tree and a strangely dressed man with an umbrella like a monk's hat came out from another card.

Several days later, during the lesson on morals, we learned about the man who was a master of calligraphy, Ono Dofu (小野道風). He was trying to improve his calligraphy by watching a frog determinedly trying to jump onto a willow bough. The red spots of the hearts, the black spots on the other cards, the iris, the peony, the spades, the black and red, all merged in front of my eyes.

But after I became an adult this image, which remained with me, clarified and divided into two; one of nature on the Korean cards, and the other of the human figures on the Western cards.

It is said that *hwat'u* was based on the idea of Western cards and made by the Japanese at the end of the sixteenth century. But as indicated in "The Devil's Picture

Book," published in New York, the *hwat'u* cards are different from Western cards and are entirely of Japanese invention. *Hwat'u*, divided into the months of the year, express the seasonal changes of nature. January pictures a pine, February, the plum and a bird, March, the cherry blossom—that is the way it starts and goes on to August with its full moon, September with the chrysanthemum, and October with the maple—all are correlated with the elegant pleasures of nature.

The Koreans, who have had strong anti-Japanese sentiments, could hardly have taken up customs of neighboring Japan.

Hwat'u is the only exception; we have enjoyed and popularized it more than the Japanese because the feeling of affinity to nature fits our taste.

Our traditional feeling of love for flowers, birds, moon and wind, shares the same elements as those depicted on the *hwat'u* cards. The plants and flowers that we sing of and enjoy season-by-season are the plum, the chrysanthemum, the iris and the maple (which are all on Korean cards).

That is, *hwat'u* may have come from Japan, but it can be said to coincide with our emotions and our life.

Western cards are, however, different from *hwat'u*. If *hwat'u* reflects a keen awareness of a harmony with nature, Western cards can be said to symbolize social consciousness and the powerful human.

One says that Western cards came from India, another says they are related to mysterious Egyptian philosophy; still, a third says that they came from T'ang China or from the gypsies; we cannot deny the fact that the cards repre-

154

sent a dramatization of the special Western image. Being different from *hwat' u,* they do not represent nature, but human society in the form of allegory (fable).

Although there are changes in terms of time and country, the pictures express the images of all sorts of things which arose from human society; jokers, a female pope, queens, kings, lovers, war chariots, righteousness, the hermit, the chariot of fate, strength, the executed, death, the devil, the house of the spirit, constellations, moon, sun, judges, the world, and the like. These days the pictures have become simple; the king and queen, diamonds (symbol of wealth), the heart (symbol of priesthood), spades (swords), clubs (agriculture). But they still symbolize the social consciousness of man.

Hwat' u, therefore, reflects nature's image, while Western cards reflect a human society.

Hwat' u and Western cards can be said to be a symbolic key to distinguish Oriental and Western history. In our hearts are engraved the pictures of the flowers and plants of *hwat' u,* not those of Western cards. We can see that Korea has been ruled more by a consciousness of nature than by human consciousness, and by the spirit of accord with nature rather than social consciousness. While the Westerner looked for glittering diamonds and flaming hearts and intended to conquer with the king and the spade, we sought the crane resting on the pine branch and appreciated the song of the bird in the shadow of the plum.

In the West the rainbow became the subject of poetry for Wordsworth, and nature appeared on the scene with Millet. They have drawn only people. What they looked for was the beauty they discovered in humanity, whether it was the image of Jesus or angels or the mysterious smile of the Gioconda. Nature was nothing but a background for humanity.

But we are the exact opposite. In the East, nature is the subject, and man is only a background. The shepherd is painted on Greek vases, but on Korean pottery it is the willow. They humanize nature and we "naturize" humanity.

We say that the woman's eyebrow is like a half moon. The eyebrow is changed into a new moon. But like T. E. Hume, they say "The moon like a farmer." The moon is changed into man. We compare man to nature, while they compare nature to man.

Like Pak In-no's *sijo* poem:

> *By the hills and waters, and under the pine a wide field*
> *The blue-green mist and the red haze, fold upon fold,*
> *Oh, Nature is a rosy-clouded screen newly drawn!*

We did not live in a human screen, but for a thousand years within the rosy, misty screen of nature.

36. Hints from
The Secret Arts of T'ojŏng

Translator's note: The T'ojŏng Pi-kyŏl (土亭秘訣), or *The Secret Arts of T'ojŭng*, is a book written by Lee Chi-ham(李之菡), who lived from 1517 to 1578. His pen name was T'ojŏng(土亭). At the time of his death he was *gunsu* of A-san gun, Ch'ungch'ŏng-namdo. This book is widely used as a guide to telling fortunes for the year, and is especially used at the beginning of the year. Its influence in Korea is still very strong.

*T*HE *Secret Arts of T'ojŏng* is a Korean best-seller. Along with *The Records of Chŏng Kam* (鄭鑑錄), it has been from olden times a work which has ruled the outlook of the masses regarding their fate. While it is not related to cultural prognostication, even today at the beginning and at the end of the year it still has a soaring sale. It seems to have some sort of attraction that captures the mind of the Korean. Even the intelligentsia, who cry out to break with superstition, open and read *The Secret Arts of T'ojŏng* at least once to divine their new year's fortune.

But what draws our interest is more the content of the discussions on fate rather than the psychology of the masses. That is to say, we must see what the character of good and evil is as it is written in *The Secret Arts of T'ojŏng*, rather than the things in it which are believed.

Even though the contents of *The Secret Arts of T'ojŏng* were written several hundred years ago, they are still in common use in modern society and the reason must be that they relate to the fate of the Koreans. As everyone knows, among the yearly fortunes which appear most frequently, the most prominent relates to "the fortune of slander and gossip" (口舌數). For example, it is written "In this month there is a fate of slander and gossip so keep your mouth closed like a bottle," or "Although there are good financial prospects, be careful of slander and gossip," or "Along with trifling things, there will be much slander and gossip" —in any divination slander and gossip are included.

If we put it another way, it means that there is a great deal of trouble in our society from gossip. Because of the damage done by words, we have evolved the habit of fearing and being careful of talk, and we can see that this kind of habit plays an important role in the divination of T'ojŏng's secret art.

Like the spilling of water from a clumsily mishandled bottle, there have been many cases where careless talk has ruined and disgraced families.

If we were to speak in modern terms, we could say that there is a prediction of slander and gossip regarding the person who gets arrested under the "Spreading False Information Law." So we feel quite keenly that traditionally our "freedom of discussion" and "constructive criticism" have been very restricted.

The recognition that words, which are the most basic means of communication among men, cause evil is proof that our human relations are not healthy. The fact that we fear men's talk can explain why we pay serious attention to the opinions of others.

Actually, from olden days we have been afraid of rumors, and our people have been overly nervous about gossip behind their backs. This fear of criticism is ingrained, and we have never accepted or taken a positive attitude towards it.

This negative mental attitude shows that people are more cautious about words than concerned with individual action; even today we have inherited this restriction on speaking without change as of old.

Although several centuries have passed since T'ojŏng died, the prophesy of "being careful about slander and gossip," even in the Korea of today, is still lively and remains a keen question.

Secondly, one of the prophesies which occurs many times is that concerning the disasters of officialdom. Examples are "Fear the devil-like officials who come close to you" or "Do not become an official, damage will be done to you" or "This month's forecast is to be careful of disaster caused by officials." Many other examples are divined and play a large part in the book. We know all about this too well without very many explanations.

We are a people who have always been oppressed by officials. Like disease, fire and unexpected accidents, the official who causes trouble for the people is one type of trouble similar to a disaster from which there is no defense. The term "disaster caused by officials" is in itself already abnormal. T'ojŏng certainly was a genius in understanding this. There is a great probability that harm from officials will befall one. This prophet knew that from the beginning a greater portion of the disasters inflicted on people were of this type.

Thirdly, many lines of forecast were written about damage from human relations. "If you are not careful of people who have the wood or metal radical in their surname, evil will befall you."[1] or "Don't make new friends" or "Don't believe your friends." These occur as warnings far more often than do exhortations to be careful about fire or water. Also, there are many instances saying not to go out with others. Everywhere it is written that one "should not go to the northeast" or "one should close the gate and not go out" or "if one takes a trip there will be trouble." Simply stated, these prognostications reflect our closed life which is lived in mistrust of human and social

---

1. Each character has a radical or element by which it may be catalogued. So the wood radical 木 includes such names as Lee or Yi 李 or Pak 朴, and the metal radical 金 is the same as the name Kim 金, to give but a few examples.

relations. Although it is sometimes written that "an unexpected and valued guest will come and bring luck," this too is a forecast of the traditional temperament of a people who expect luck through relying on others, rather than on their own work.

When we read *The Secret Arts of T'ojŏng*, we may presume from it our traditional human and social relations. In fact, that *The Secret Arts of T'ojŏng* in modern society has not lost its mysterious power, finally proves that the past and present share the same destiny.

Although we have succeeded in loving nature, following nature's laws, and assimilating ourselves to nature, the destiny stated in *The Secret Arts of T'ojŏng* about the evils of gossip, officials and personal relations shows that the fact is we have failed in loving mankind, in building order in human relations and in communicating smoothly with other people.

There has been a lack of human recognition. T'ojŏng advised us to be careful about speech, officials, friends and going out. But also people thought that T'ojŏng was right. I guess that this is not really superstition, but rather a sort of science of probability. In Korean society everyone must face these issues. Today, also, the wrinkled faces of the Koreans who sit and read *The Secret Arts of T'ojŏng* cast the dark shadow of one hundred years past and one hundred years in the future.

Author's note: Chŏng Kam wrote a book of prophesy in the early Yi Dynasty. It consists of a dialogue between Chŏng Kam and Yi Sim. If *The Secret Arts of T'ojŏng* is one of the books of prophesy concerning individual fate, *The Records of Chŏng Kam* is a book of prophesy concerning the historical and social fate of the whole people.

The Records of Chŏng Kam, as in the case of *The Secret Arts of T'ojŏng,* is a story mainly concerned with evil. It is full of escape to nature to avoid evil; for example, it tells where to find shelter to avoid destruction and the rise and fall of the nation. It is the kind of material by which we can deduce what the Koreans' social and historical viewpoint was.

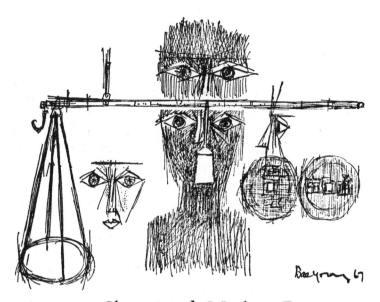

37. Shops and Market Days

THE Korean term *kage* (가게) means a shop. But originally it was the word *kaga* which meant a temporary shack (假家), a slap-dash hut like the squatter's shacks of today. Later the sound changed and *kaga* became *kage*. We scorn shops as something which won't quite do, as in the proverb "Pasting up poetry welcoming spring on the pillars of a shop"—such verses should only be put up on a home of some prominence.

So why do we indicate a shop by using the term for a temporary shack? If we search out the origins of this term, we will find that we were completely uninterested in commerce.

In Western European society, from the period before

the Middle Ages, m arkets flourished. Everyone knows that Phoenicia was famous as a trading nation. It even seems that the three wise men who came from the east bringing gifts of frankincense, myrrh and gold at the time of Christ's birth were middle-eastern traders. Cities grew up along waterways and merchants were able to transport goods freely. These were the sea traders. It is a fact which is widely known and documented that the scope of the medieval French international market place of Champagne was wonderfully great and luxurious.

But in Korea during the Yi Dynasty, by the close of the fourteenth century, there were scarcely any markets. It seems that there was no market function. There was not enough sense of trading goods. As Lee Hang-bok said, whenever the occasion required it in the court, the officials would take whatever they needed from the traders in the market place. While they called it commerce, it was commerce in name only; actually they took away these goods by compulsion and without payment.

It was not only the government which did this, but the upper-class *yangban* who had power and carried out private trade. They thought of the shops of others as their own warehouses, and it seems that they took and used these things as they wanted.

The traders themselves did not pay their taxes. They would form wholesale houses for itinerant traders, give money or goods to avoid paying taxes, get a monopoly on goods and raise and lower prices as they wished. When the market system became confused, houses were built on sidestreets and temporary stores were opened. These were the so-called temporary shacks (假家). The reason that they were not houses built in the regular way was that such employment was not stabilized.

The so-called temporary shacks or stores were not legal and were called "haphazard stores." Sometimes, if they wanted, officials would come after these stores and tear them down. So, as they didn't know when the shops would be torn down and when they would be shut, it was more fitting to build them of planks. If we think about it, the so-called hole-in-the-wall shops and box-like shops of today, which are also often torn down in confusion, are nothing but a repetition of the tradition of the old days.

In our country commerce did not become a free enterprise system until the opening of Korea. In other words, we would not put it too strongly if we said that the budding of the recognition of commerce came together with contact with Western civilization.

If we look at a rural market-day scene this becomes obvious. Originally, the origins of the market, as we have said, were similar to some sort of celebration more than to commerce. The rural wives would wait for the return of their husbands who brought them face powder or an imitation silk which they had bought. The children's hearts would jump with joy from the time the father measured their feet with rice straw; they would get a new pair of rubber shoes.

Traders would get flushed from drinking *makkŏli* and, treading on their own shadows in the moonlight, would return home, perhaps singing the phrase of some song. They had no cash, but they would go with the products they had so carefully made or the handicrafts they had produced so laboriously or the ten eggs they had wrapped in straw. The Korean market was thus the buying and selling of what they had made with their own emotions.

John Carver said that trade was competition in deception. One blinds someone else's eyes and muffles his hearing to gather gold like King Midas. Koreans have thought that traders are base and that this job is the lowest in a society which ranks the scholar on top, followed by the farmer, the artisan and lastly the merchant.

And though the markets in the West where things were bought and sold were often quite naturally scenes of violence, only the Korean market place was one in which warm human emotions whirled about. These days things have changed and the cold wind of commercialism blows, with swindlers trying to change prices and cheat people. But even today we can still see in the Korean market place the Korean sentiment lingering like the afterglow at sunset. Educated Korean hermits kept their distance from hard-hearted commercialism because they didn't like the inhuman nature of materialism and such a heartless sense of existence.

But because they were careless about trade, so great was their isolation from society, communications between people became poorer. So economic power and social circulation declined. Like the snail, they only lived within their shell and a greater sense of humanity could not develop.

Merchants are more than a bridge between producers and consumers. They are a stepping stone to the expanse of the general populace in which human beings exchange views with each other and communicate. From here a sense of public morality begins. But we Koreans were lonely and desolate and vacant like the closing of the market. We could not find in Korea the great markets in which the power of life draws crowds, vitality, people clashing with each other, and flames and vital existence.

If we say that the traders who dominated Western society were like animals, then the educated hermits who controlled our society were like vegetables.

Author's note: In the Yi Dynasty essays of Ch'u Kang (秋江令話), there is a discussion of the origins of the market. The Kyŏngsang Province people in March, April and May chose one day for making offerings to the mountain god. The wealthy brought barley in carts and the poor carried it on their backs to display before the spirit. For three days they played the bamboo flute and drums and ate and drank. Then they returned home after the offering and they bartered their goods. Without this type of service to the god, they could not barter.

Now in our country our morality of commerce is not sufficient. Our talk about using a "one-price" system proves that we lack such morality. And if we read *The History of Korea* by Lee Sang-ok, there is one episode which describes how Korea's commerce was not prosperous:

"At the time of the Imjin War (1592), foreigners thought that Korea had no merchants and so the government told the people to make a market to show the Chinese of the Ming Dynasty that Korea had prosperous trade. But the people didn't have any goods to sell so they brought out the furniture and goods they used in daily life and displayed them in the market and sat for a while. Then afterwards they returned home in the afternoon carrying their belongings."

167

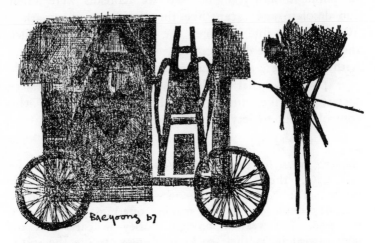

38. Lament on the A-Frame

AMERICANS call the *chige* (지게) the A-frame, the reason being that the shape of the *chige* is just like the shape of the letter A. Of course, the A-frame does not exist in the United States. American troops came to Korea and saw our A-frame and simply gave it this name. It reminded them of the letter A, although in our hearts we know it is much more complicated. We know too well the varied content, the sighs and the annoyances all mixed together in the A-frame.

The A-frame, needless to say, is a tool which is used to carry things on the back. But more than a tool, it is something which flows in our blood and feelings. From the A-frame emanates the smell of sweat which is just the body odor of the Korean.

First there is the shape itself. The A-frame is not man made. Because it is made of tree branches which are in the shape of an A, there is not a trace of a hammer or a nail in it. Even the stick which supports the A-frame is cut from a Y-shaped branch.

The A-frame actually has many uses. Wherever a man is able to go, it can accompany him. It is not only something which is necessary to carry baggage; the A-frame is the farmer's natural musical instrument. While hitting the leg of the A-frame with a stick, he sings the "woodcutters song" in accompaniment to this rhythm while he goes along the lonely and quiet path between the rice fields. It is the farmer's best, consoling friend.

So too, the A-frame is the farmer's comfortable chair. He lays it down and rests his tired body on it. The face of the farmer who is napping on the A-frame is more peaceful than that of a gentleman asleep in his armchair.

The A-frame is the woodcutter's heart. In the spring it is decorated with azaleas, in summer with wild vines and berries, and in fall with red maple leaves. I would choose the woodcutter's A-frame over the beautifully decorated bride's dressing table.

What about the stick which goes with the A-frame? In the old days the Japanese or Europeans walked carrying a sword. But to the very tame rural Korean farmer, this stick is a unique weapon. When some emergency occurs, he immediately picks up the stick and gives chase. Like the Caduceus of Hermes, it symbolizes infinite abilities.

We cannot explain the life of the Korean living in our soil without the A-frame. There is a great mission for the A-frame in real life beyond these romantic reasons. Yet, there is profound sorrow and suffering about it too. It is symbolic of our very cruel fate.

What meaning is there in the A-frame which is the unique product of Korea? If our ancestors themselves made any creative invention, it was the A-frame. We are not complaining because the A-frame is not as worthy a discovery as the automobile. We only complain because they preferred the A-frame to wider paths. There must have been carts. They had wagons too, but they made A-frames for those too many narrow paths where wagons couldn't go. Instead of widening the paths, they adjusted themselves to the narrow ones which already existed.

We may say that the A-frame was produced simply to fit our actual situation rather than our having given positive thought to solving our reality. So we do not exaggerate if we say that the A-frame is a symbol of all the tragedy of Korea.

An ignorant negro may push a "chariot" or cart, and even our neighbors, the Chinese, carry things in a wheelbarrow. They made roads for the wagons, while we didn't even have the concept of "a road." We only had paths through the mountains which were produced naturally and on which we walked—paths reminiscent of the old Korean poem "How tortuous it is to follow the numerous curves winding like sheep's intestines!" We call our modern roads literally "newly made roads" proving that formerly we had no real roads. Our roads, one might say, are those which have just been installed since modernization. Before then there were no roads except narrow paths meandering through the mountains over which even wagons found it difficult to pass.

Roads are a social measure of communication between men and a symbol of culture. A society without roads means an isolated society. Rome's prosperity began with her roads. As they say, "All roads lead to Rome." Rome's citizens acquired the world through making roads. When I go towards you, and when you come towards me, we do so by roads. Roads are cooperation and unity.

So, as we try to walk on these slender rural passages carrying our A-frame, we feel a similar kind of constrained passage of thought. As we see the farmer climbing up and down the slopes of the hills carrying such a heavy load on his A-frame, we also see the suffering of all Koreans who pant on the dangerous slope of the path carrying the heavy historical load of a thousand years piled high on their shoulders.

We have to ask ourselves today, and not just ask the graves of our ancestors, why didn't we make roads instead of making the A-frame, and why didn't we make roads to fit us, rather than fitting ourselves to the roads? Thus every Korean carries on his shoulders an invisible A-frame —this A·frame of subservience to nature.

Some people say that, given our present situation which is like our roads, carrying out democracy is difficult. They say we should make our democracy, like our A-frame, fit us. These people don't think of making a road by changing our actual situation so that the carriage of freedom can pass. People say, "let us use dictatorship like our heavy A-frame on the steep path"—this is the type of thinking which I fear.

39. Walking to the Right or Left?

Translator's note: This chapter illustrates the influence of Confucianism on Korean society. Readers are invited to refer to the Confucian classic *The Doctrine of the Mean,* which describes "the middle way."

DID the people of the olden days walk to the left or the right when they went out into the street? Historians often play with this problem which never leaves them bored. Of course, traffic patterns in the old days didn't come into being as a preventative against accidents caused by wheeled vehicles. The point is that there weren't any cars, and when one met an enemy, one just employed whatever method of defense seemed most useful without regard to whether one moved right or left.

Historians declare, however, that from the Middle Ages Western society basically has kept to the left. Traders

172

and travelers, not to mention royalty, carried swords or spears. If an enemy or a robber appeared suddenly, the left side was more advantageous than the right because in order to draw a sword with the right hand, the adversary had to stand to the right. So these historians say that the pattern of traffic at that time was to walk on the left. This old habit remains even today, and people still walk to the left.

Only America follows a different pattern, and there people walk to the right. This is because the American frontiersmen didn't carry swords but guns instead. In the West, at the time of the invention of firearms, public security had been achieved and there was no need to carry arms; only the situation on the American frontier was different. As we see in cowboy movies, because it was a lawless land where savage Indians ambushed people too often, even in the period of firearms people had to carry weapons.

In a word, the gun was different from the sword in that it was faster to draw the former than the latter and more advantageous to assault from right to left. It is said, therefore, that they have firmly kept the custom of walking to the right.

What about the Koreans, then. Did they walk to the left or right? Unfortunately historians have not been able to offer a clear explanation except in the saying "The superior man (君子) walks on the wide road."

If we today observe the habit of rural elders walking on the road, perhaps we can get a clear idea of what happened in the past. Examine the walking habit of the old rural gentlemen—these gentlemen never care whether they walk to the right or the left as their white beards dance in the wind and their toes point outwards like the Chinese character for eight(八).

Moreover, they don't have to look around nervously like a sparrow worried about who might attack them. They just walk imperturbably in the center of the road. Basically they have no sense of confrontation.

That's just it. The Korean, that superior man, clearly chose the center of the road. Of course there was no difference on a narrow lane between right and left, but we cannot deny that they chose the middle. As indicated in the introduction to this book, when they are frightened and run away, country people still take to the middle of the road.

The superior man of the old days would stand with awkward hesitation when a robber confronted him on the road. He had no habit of attacking robbers with sword or spear. Hence there was no need to employ a sense of right or left. They believed it was proper to face unavoidable emergencies in the center. To talk about left or right is a habit of nervous Europeans and the Japanese.

Lack of strict maintenance of a traffic order can be ascribed to the lack of public consciousness and to the temper of the hermit who dislikes arguing.

It is not only in the custom of walking, but in the way of thinking; the special trait of the Korean is not to be inclined towards any one side.

Its cause may be ascribed to a long training based on Confucianism. But it may be better to say that it was congenial to our nature to choose the middle way to avoid all extremes. The intellectual history of the West has

174

developed by solving the problem of how to avoid dilemmas. The Westerners are a people who, in a situation where there are conflicting values, must choose one of them. But the Koreans are not especially annoyed by a sense of contradiction. The people who shed tears for the students who shed blood to eliminate Syngman Rhee applauded and cried when Syngman Rhee left the presidential mansion to move into his private residence. This is the Korean temperament of one who walks on the middle path without feeling any contradiction in the two streams of tears, one for Syngman Rhee and one against him.

The legend of the "filial-unfilial bridge" illustrates this. In the Silla period there was a widow who, while her sons slept, would cross the Kyo river to visit her lover. Her seven sons knew about this and, as they worried whether their mother might get sick crossing the cold water, built a bridge. Then the mother repented her unchaste act and stopped her rendezvous. But the people named that bridge the "filial-unfilial bridge," because the act of the seven sons was considered filial on the one hand and unfilial on the other. They didn't suffer by taking this contradictory action. They just called it the "filial-unfilial bridge." Their attitude was one of loving and accepting contradictions without analyzing them. Herein lies the hesitating and awkward gait of the Korean.

Author's note: By an open mind we mean one which has the generosity of being able to accept contradictions. As an example, we have a story about a Korean official of the old days named Hwang Hi. One day he heard each side of the story of two men who were fighting. He answered both separately that they were each right. A third man overheard this and asked him, "How come you said that both were right? Since they are fighting, one or the other must be right." Hwang Hi answered, "You too are right."

40. A History Without Toys

IN Lee Sang's essay *Ennui* he includes a story of rural children lining up and defecating by the side of the road in a kind of game brought on through boredom.

Whenever we observe Korean children, we get a sort of tightness in our chests from remembering both the funny and the sad scenes of that *ennui*. Actually, Korean children are more bored and lonely than the children of any other country. They are children who have grown up in this earth and in that wind.

Adults never made toys for them. They didn't have the things of which dreams are made—the lead soldiers or the paper castles or the firecrackers or the horns and all the other things Western children have. Giving toys to our children is a recent custom, the result of modernization.

In Korea, originally there were no toys. The Japanese researcher on Korea, Mr. Yanagi, once made this point. Yet, toys already flourished from the Edo Period in nearby Japan. Both the kind and the quality were of a wonderful level. The so-called Imperial Palace Toys were developed with special ornaments which were painted in rainbow colors.

Today Japan produces 60,000 kinds of toys and toy export in one year is worth one billion yen. Japan is the world leader in the production of toys; they almost have a monopoly on foreign trade in toys as well as supplying their own people.

In the West from prehistoric times there have been toys, and from the tombs of ancient Egypt toy soldiers and slaves have been excavated.

Of course, though they were not purely children's toys, the tradition of toys in the West is an old one. However poor the home, if there are children, there will be toys, even if it is only a wooden doll.

Why is our country the only one without toys? In Korea there is something called the *norikae* (노리개), but that is more a body ornament for adults than for children. Thus Korean children themselves were the ones who had to make their own toys with their own hands. If the toys weren't made out of watermelon rind thrown away by adults or made out of broken glass, then the children would pick up round stones and use them as toys. With rice husks they made crude puppets, with the stem of the pepper plant an A-Frame, and with corn stalks a horse. But whatever the children did, the adults were not concerned. No, lack of concern is not it. If the children by chance made a grass puppet, the adults would tie it up with a rope of twisted straw and throw it in the latrine because they felt it would bring bad luck.

Finally, that there were no toys in our country means that concern for children was lacking. And a lack of concern for children can be said to be a lack of vision for the future. It seems that we live in the present more than the future and in the past more than the present.

Ours is a country where everything is "past centered." Whoever we are, we like talking about the past. All discussions end with the expression "Ah, the good old days, Ah, the good old days." As if everyone lived well in the past and all was wonderful!

Countries are just the same. While we get flour and pressed barley from the Americans, whose history is not more than a couple of hundred years old, we still never forget to boast about our "five millenia of glorious history."

If we stop and ask a beggar on the street, he will boast telling us the story of his eighth generation ancestor who was governor of Pyŏng An. But if you ask about his present or future situation, he will answer effortlessly "Somehow we will manage to live" or "Cobwebs don't grow on a living mouth."

The people of Bismark Island in New Ireland draw a picture of the face of their dead relative or friend and after six months they make a mask and have a memorial parade. But we live with our memorial parade throughout the year.

We look out at the world through the face of the past. Whether in mirth or in sadness, we share our emotion with our dead ancestors. On ceremonial days we visit our ancestors' tombs and though we cannot remember the dead, when the anniversary of the death comes around we light incense at the ancestral shrine. We live with someone's death mask. Although it is a beautiful custom, it gives the impression we are slaves to the past. So too, time for living and planning for the future is absent. That idea is found in the proverb "Even though you want to eat well on your birthday, you cannot go hungry and save up for it today."

André Maurois complained that the French farmer saved too much for the future. What the French farmer produced he put in his sock. We do not invest in the future; we cannot find any savings here. If there is anything, we eat it up. In a society where there are no guarantees for the future, a high rate of expenditure is not unreasonable.

History is a bed. To those who lie on it, it is necessary; but to those who are active, it is quite different. The American frontiersmen only lived for the future. Also, when we examine their literary figures, such as Mark Twain, there are many children as protagonists in their novels; and if we examine the American family structure, it is child-centered, which is quite different from ours. But we are a people blind to the future, who knew how to erect stone pillars at our ancestors' graves but didn't think about making toys for children. A history without toys; it is a history without a future.

Bae young 67

41. Trains and Rebellion

ALTHOUGH trains come and go every day, in rural areas children never treat them as routine. When they hear the warning whistle on their way home from school, they put their book bags on their shoulders and run to the rails. The black train appears between the spurs of the hills, pouring forth smoke. The children silently line up in a row and wait for the train to approach.

What on earth do they want to do? One... two... three... the carriages pass by right in front of their eyes. There are the faces of the strange travellers looking out of the windows. Then the children, as if planned, together raise their hands and make obscene gestures.

No doubt that while this type of abuse is a joke, their appearance is serious, like that of a rural stationmaster's businesslike behavior. Until the train has disappeared, the children continue making these obscene gestures, panting all the while. It is a strange habit.

It is not only the children who act this way. The adults cultivating the rice paddies or the fields stop their work when the train passes and do similar things. When one man loudly cries out, "What kind of guys are they to have such good luck to ride the train," the lament is answered, "We can never get out of our miserable situation."

But when we see foreign movies, they show a scene of marked contrast. When trains pass through farming areas, the children gather together and shout "bravo" and the farmers wave at the travellers.

It is true that Korea's modernization was extended through the railroads which were built during the Japanese occupation; but this does not necessarily mean the flourishing of a new culture. With this new wave has come a different and obscure reaction of great significance.

The train transports those who use the products of this new flourishing culture, the modernized stick and spectacles which are the cane and the eyeglasses. So too, those who wore Western clothes—the clerk of the subcounty office and the Japanese policeman from the branch police box—took the train. And they only made trouble for the farmers.

Because Korean modernization emerged together with her history as a colony, this kind of flourishing was seen as a symbol of guilt and oppression.

Many sad and pitiful events take place at the lonely rural railway station where the coxcomb and the cosmos bloom—such as when the young country girls leave to be sold as servants or prostitutes in Seoul, or when one's neighbors leave their old home forever with their gourd dipper as their only baggage. Also, it was the train which took away the emigrants to Osaka, in Japan, or Manchuria.

Yi Hyo-sŏk's[1] novel *Pig* has similar scenes. The train separated Puni and her tame pig from her lover, and this scene at the railway station did not disappear easily from the mind of the rural young man who continued to stare at the train. This illustrates the depth of his frustration.

Listening to the sentimental popular song in which "the train departs in the drizzle," or the folk song in which "the 'high collar'[2] arrogant guys order everyone around" and others, we can presume the opposition and the sad feeling towards the railroad

In the humorous action of the children who make these obscene gestures at the train we can read the rebellious hearts of the Koreans towards modernization. Rebellion of this sort is insignificant. The most they can do is give dirty looks to the end of the train or shake their fists. We can also say that this is superficial opposition towards things like trains or Western clothes more than it is rebellion towards anything basic.

Fundamentally, the rebellion of the Korean is more emotional than logical, and intermittent rather than continuous. As the weather in Korea is three days of cold followed by four days of warmth,[3] rebellion appears to be fitful, such as the rebellion against King Sejo,[4] or the

---

1. Yi Hyo-sŏk (1907–1940) was a modern writer famous mainly for his short stories.
2. "High collar" refers to those Koreans who cooperated with the Japanese and were "modernized," which was characterized by their wearing of Western clothes and white shirts with high collars. It was a term of approbation.
3. This is a common folk saying about Korean winter weather.
4. The seventh king of the Yi Dynasty (reigned 1456–1468).

March 1st, 1919 Independence Movement, or the April 19, 1960 Student Rebellion.

Koreans remain calm and then suddenly rebel. They then are once again subdued. It is not the kind of rebellion which is continuous like bitter cold; but it may be said that it is a rebellion of the "three days cold and four days warm" variety in which warmth and cold alternate.

Although Hong Kil-tong(洪吉童) was an uncommon rebel who challenged social evils and formed the Hwalbin Party(活貧黨),[5] his rebellion was also similar to the emotional rebellion of making obscene gestures at trains. This novel did not develop into a revolution of the masses. The Hwalbin Party may be characterized as a party of Robin Hoods or righteous thieves.

Im Kŏk-chŏng(林巨正)[6] was the same. He robbed from the rich and gave to the poor. While this can be considered as righteous, it was not productive. If there were no rich, then the cause for rebellion would have disappeared. It was a rebellion which was unproductive. In the strict sense this is animosity more than rebellion, and closer to envy than to animosity.

We ourselves at this moment are experiencing the fact that this envy does not develop into real social rebellion, and becomes nothing more than an example of simple discontent. Rebellion and envy are different, as are criticism and complaint. The making of obscene gestures at trains shows that the Korean rebellion is envy.

---

5. Hong Kil-tong is a ficticious folk character from an old Yi Dynasty novel. He was a sort of folk superman who formed the Hwalbin or Save-the-poor Party. His exploits are still popular today. They appear on television and in movies.
6. Im Kŏk-chŏng was another legendary Yi Dynasty figure.

Rae-yorang 67

42. Ch'unhyang and Helen

Translator's note: Ch'unhyang Chŏn, or the story of the Fragrance of Spring, is the most popular classic folk tale in Korea. Ch'unhyang, the daughter of an aristocrat and a *kisaeng*, lives in Namwŏn. She falls in love and secretly marries Yi Mong-yong, the son of an official. He is called to Seoul and later returns to Namwon as a secret emissary of the king, where he saves the loyal Ch'unhyang from further torture by the rapacious evil governor, Pyŏn Hak-to, who had unsuccessfully attempted to seduce her. It is an enduring tale of marital fidelity, famous in classical Korean song and story. Two Western-style operas have been written by Koreans on this theme, one has been written by a Japanese, and there is one musical comedy in English.

HELEN is the symbol of feminine beauty in the West

as described in Homer's epic poem *The Iliad*. Her beauty caused the shedding of the blood of so many, from the hero Achilles to tens of thousands of soldiers.

Although Helen originally was the queen of the Greek Menelaus, the Trojan prince Paris secretly abducted her and made her his wife. But the Greeks, to regain the beautiful Helen, invaded Troy and so started the ten year struggle which swallowed some thousands of lives. Actually this Trojan War was only fought for the beauty, Helen.

The comparison of our own Ch'unhyang with Helen should make us somewhat ashamed, as the scale is quite different. Although all the Greek heroes and soldiers suffered hardships and their lives hung in the balance until Helen was returned to the arms of Menelaus, it took just the sound of yelling the few words "The secret agent has come!" to again seat Ch'unhyang by the side of Yi Mong-yong, her husband. Everything was solved with a horse emblem.[1] There is quite a difference between the ten years of the Trojan War and the ten seconds of Ch'unhyang.

Also, though both beauties were recaptured through the crucial role played by horses—in the case of Helen through the swift soldiers who entered the Trojan horse, and with Ch'unhyang through the horse pictured on the *map' ai*, or horse emblem—how different the two are!

---

1. The *map' ai* (馬牌) was a bronze or wooden seal having on one side the picture of from one to five horses, indicating the degree of authority of the carrier, and on the other the date and seal of the Ministry concerned. Upon presentation, the owner's authority was clearly established even though he might be disguised in the clothes of a beggar.

But there is absolutely no difference of degree in our thinking of Ch'unhyang as a portrait of beauty and the Westerners in their elevation of Helen to the same position.

In comparing the Westerners' conception of beauty with our own, there is clearly a contrast between Helen and Ch'unhyang. Actually, we cannot find the slightest element of fidelity in Helen. When Paris took Helen and made her queen of Troy, Helen did not resist but followed of her own will. And after Paris was defeated and died in battle, she returned to the arms of her old husband, Menelaus.

If we were to be critical, we could say that there is no difference between Helen and a prostitute. Because of Helen, many of the Greek army lost their lives and, though she may have felt sorry, she didn't talk especially about the ten years during which she shared a bed with Paris.

If we were to make comparisons, Ch'unhyang's chastity is wonderful. Compare Ch'unhyang's attitude, kneeling on the execution ground with hair dishevelled for not favoring Governor Pyŏn Hak-to with her body, and Helen's posture, quietly looking down from the watchtower on the city walls while below on the battlefield the two armies are shedding blood and men are falling.

The elders of Troy are said to have exclaimed upon seeing the beautiful figure of Helen appear on the watchtower. Of course, they did not regret this battle. Their sons did not die in vain. . . .

The beauty of the Westerner stands above morality and is superior to reality. Beauty alone is sufficient. Talking of Helen as a beauty does not interfere with saying that because of Helen war broke out and that chastity was nothing to her.

It was not Troy's elders but the Korean elders who exclaimed upon seeing Ch'unhyang kneeling on the execution field. This exclamation was not only about a consciousness of beauty; morality, which cannot be separated from beauty, is mixed together with it. Ch'unhyang's beauty and her fidelity in not taking more than one husband cannot be separated. Koreans look at beauty differently from Westerners, who think of beauty only as beauty. To us, morality and realistic consciousness are contained in beauty.

This is the difference between Helen and Ch'unhyang. It is also the basic difference between the Korean and the Western concept of the appreciation of beauty. Our ancestors considered nature—the bamboo, the pine and the chrysanthemum—beautiful. The bamboo was beautiful because it was straight, the pine because it was evergreen, and the chrysanthemum because it alone bloomed in the frost.

Though the rose of the Westerner has thorns, it may still be beautiful; but to us even though it is lovely, that is not enough. Flowers are also elevated by symbolic morality. We know this from reading "Songs of Five Friends" by Yun Sŏn-to[2] or the song of the chrysanthemum which is compared to a faithful retainer. So to us goodness is beauty and evil ugliness. Some poet also

---

2. Yun Sŏn-to (尹善道, 1587–1671) was considered to be the greatest of *sijo* poets. The complete translation of his "Songs of Five Friends," translated by Peter H. Lee in his *Anthology of Korean Poetry,* is on page 190.

made this point. So we also say in Korean that an evil person is "a bad one" or "a filthy guy" or "a dirty or hateful guy." On the other hand, when young children do something good, we say that they are "pretty" or "cute." The characteristic of the nature of Korean beauty is in the combination of morality and beauty.

It is thus understandable that to us Ch'unhyang appears as the most idealistic beauty. As in the case of Helen, personality is ignored in the West and only beauty is sought. This attitude has produced the so-called "decadent" writers of the world, such as Oscar Wilde and Beaudelaire; their distress was that beauty and morality, and beauty and actuality were always discordant. Sometimes in the West, in extreme cases, morality even kills beauty and beauty kills reality. But Korea's traditional beauty is one which does not conflict with morality and reality; they go together.

Even today when we see beauty we say "It has style" (lit. it is similar) and "It is sort of nice" (lit. it is comparable). This just means that it is close to reality and acceptable to morality. We can say that these intimate our concept of beauty.

SONGS OF FIVE FRIENDS

How many friends have I? Count them:
Water and stone, pine and bamboo—
The rising moon on the east mountain,
Welcome, it too is my friend.
What need is there, I say,
To have more friends than five

They say clouds are fine; I mean the color
But, alas, they often darken.
They say winds are clear; I mean the sound.
But, alas, they often cease to blow.
It is only the water, then,
That is perpetual and good.

Why do flowers fade so soon
Once they are in their glory?
Why do grasses yellow so soon
Once they have grown tall?
Perhaps it is the stone, then,
That is constant and good.

Flowers bloom when it is warm:
Leaves fall when days are cool.
But, O pine, how is it
That you scorn frost, ignore snow?
I know now your towering self,
Straight even among the Nine Springs.

You are not a tree, no,
Nor a plant, not even that.
Who let you shoot so straight; what
Makes you empty within?
You are green in all seasons,
Welcome, bamboo, my friend.

Small but floating high,
You shed light on all creation.
And what can match your brightness
In the coal dark of the night?
You look at me but with no words;
That's why, O moon, you are my friend.

Translated by Peter H. Lee

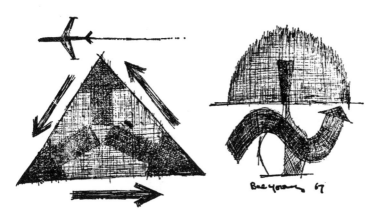

Bae young 67

43. The Pyramids and the Five Kings' Tombs of Silla

ISN'T there a great deal of difference between the Egyptian pyramids and the tombs of the Silla kings even though they are alike in that they are royal tombs? The appearance of the pyramids which stand erect in the rough and endless desert bespeaks of a powerful human will. As in the name "pyramid," it is the straight line of a spindle which stretches upward, like the point of a needle standing sharply perpendicular, as if to penetrate the sky; a cold feeling is evoked by this unemotional pile of rocks. The pyramids reveal the resistance of a people who scorned sadness. One feels the man-made power which challenges all life and even heaven and earth.

But if we look at the five tombs of the Silla kings which appear like natural mountains wrapped in a curving

191

line, we feel stillness, tranquility and warmth. We think of the gentle earth, the green grass and the flowing curve of a parabola like a sea swell; although they are great and magnificent like a range of mountains, they do not give us any oppressive feeling.

In them we sense an emotion full of life, as cozy as rubbing one's cheek against one's mother's breast.

If the beauty of the pyramids lies in their straight line, the beauty of the five royal tombs of Silla lies in their curves. We can see the contrast of character not only between the straight line and the rounded line, between the stone and the grass, but between geometric beauty and palpitating beauty.

Generally, Western art, like that of the Arabs, is largely geometric. They discovered the straight line, as in the axiom "The straight line is the shortest distance between two points," and in it they have created their own civilization. As Cezanne said, the straight line is man-made and artificial. Nature always abhors the straight line. The floating clouds, the winding streams, the branches and leaves of the trees-all living and natural things are curved.

But the straight line, like the pyramids, expresses power through man's creation; the bridge across a stream, the pavement on which cars run, the railroad, the square buildings shaped like matchboxes, telephone poles and factory chimneys, and the modern cities which are lined like a *paduk* board—all are connected with straight lines. We can say that the heart itself is a straight line.

We can say that Western civilization has replaced the natural curve with the mechanistic straight line. They

192

have turned the curved roads into *autobahns* and highways, and as if this weren't enough, they have finally come to depend upon the airplane which flies in an endless straight line. The airplane is the victory of the straight line over the curve. However much they dig tunnels and make bridges, the roads cannot always be straight; they are blocked in the end by the curve of nature. But as Saint Exupery (1900-1944) testified, the airplane taught man the absolute straight line.

If the straight line symbolizes the beauty of motion, will, challenge, pragmatism and materialism, then the curve can be said to represent the beauty of stillness, emotion, obedience, leisure and a sense of spirituality.

The characteristic beauty of Korea, as in the five tombs of the Silla kings, lies in its curves. There are delicate and slender curves and long, long curves wherever the touch and breath of the Koreans are.

Mr. Yu Chong-yŏl has said that Korean art is an art of line, especially the beauty of the curve. Look down at Seoul city from Namsan. Roof after roof flow in waves of endless curves. If there are any roofs which break this principle, they are either Western houses or Japanese houses.

Mr. Yu has offered the following reason why Koreans try to find beauty in curved lines: Among the countries of this region, China is the continent, Japan the island and Korea the peninsula. Characteristic of the first was peaceful living on earth, of the second, enjoyment of life, and of Korea, flight from the earth. The first had power, the second enjoyment, and the third loneliness. The first one with power chose form, the second color, and the third line. The one with power was adored and respected, the second tasted happiness, and the third received sympathy. As Korean history was one of anguish, a life soaked with sadness, Koreans had to depend on the lonely line which yearns for the other shore and consolation.

The bell of the Pongdŏk Temple, the waist of the observatory of Kyŏngju built during Silla times, the curved roof of the Korean house, the swaying willow branch and "waterbirds behind the willow" (a characteristic Korean design), the neck of the slender long wine bottle, the Buddha statues, the stone pagodas, the fans, the paths through the rice fields, and even the straw sandals and the rubber shoes—all express a lonely desire to fulfill in the present world wishes which can not be satisfied in an everlasting curve.

In the beauty of this curve like the stains of tears lies the Korean emotion which attempts to secretly console the bruised heart.

Indeed, it is difficult to find in Korea the "form" of the reliable Chinese or the "color" of the Japanese who try to enjoy life. Nor is there a straight line like a pyramid representing the strong will to cross the desert. The ghastly beauty of the vine-like curve—this may be the heart of these people who have stealthily suffered hunger and maltreatment but preserved their identity intact.

Line is a slender outline which separates nonexistence and another kind of nonexistence. The beauty of line is an unsubstantial beauty without reality.

Author's note: If we compare the vineyards of Alsace, Burgundy and Champagne with the paths between the rice fields in Korea, we can see the difference. As Arman Perant said, the vineyard is always in a straight line while the ricefield paths are always curved. Western ballet is more the movement and beauty of the straight line, while the Korean dance is a movement of the curved line, closer to a circle. As Herbert Read says, "The beauty of line is in every farming country, for it is basically a characteristic of farmer's folk art." Korea belongs to such a farming population, hence it is not alone in the world of arts which emphasizes line.

Baeyongs 67

44. The Gourd and the Beauty of Form

THE gourd is one of a few objects with which the Koreans have a special relationship. We plant a gourd beside the wall or by the back fence not for the practical reason of having the vines grow over them. In the poor life of the rural people the gourd is both a romantic luxury and an important asset. When the green vine grows around a dilapidated thatched hut, it never looks shabby. The gourd gives quite a different feeling from the wisteria of the luxurious Western-style mansions.

The gourd's beautiful white flower blooms in the moonlight; it is also interesting to see the gourd growing day by day like the attractive full moon. Both the flower and the gourd emit simple elegance.

When the season is over, the gourd hardens. As it ripens, so do the expectations of the rural wives. The gourd is a gift from heaven which gives joy the year around. Small or large, it has various uses. The farmers pick one especially large and well-ripened and make it into what is called a "lucky gourd." The lucky characters "long life, luck, health and peace" or "wealth and many sons" are written on it and it is given to the daughter as her possession when she is to be married.

We cannot count the uses of the gourd either as a toy or as an indispensable object in daily life. It is used as a measuring tool, like the *twe* (되), to measure rice and as a mask in the masked dance plays. At the well it becomes a dipper; on the farm it becomes a bowl for rice or food.

In the favorite Korean story about two brothers, Hŭngbu and Nolbu, the gourd plays an important role. In it is the dream of the Korean miracle which brings happiness to the good but poor person. The gourd is the Korean Messiah which brings joy to Hŭngbu but cold chills to Nolbu.

What we have to focus our attention on, however, is that the gourd symbolizes the beauty of a form which the Korean loves.

We love an oval shape, like a gourd, which has slight irregularities and which is plain, rounded and wide. The thin and elongated handle when hollowed out, the simple yet somewhat unbalanced and natural volume— nowhere does it look uneven or nervously angled. We can say that the archetype of Korean beauty might be founded in the shape of the gourd, demure and simple yet with a hidden variety. Koreans don't like women's faces to be sharp and cubistic. They think that such faces are crafty, virtueless and inauspicious. Hence, their ideal face is round and natural, like the gourd which brings luck.

Pottery keeps to the original form of a gourd. The Grecian urn that Keats almost went out of his mind to praise is conical-shaped like a modern cocktail glass. But in Korean pottery the bottom is round and the neck at the top is slender, like a gourd set upside down. The contour of the shape is like the oblong gourd. The subtle shape of the gourd breathes primitive naturalness untouched by man. This is especially true of earthenware.

Not only pottery, but the small bag, the button of the men's jackets, the comma-shaped beads, the brazier, the grave, the head of Maitreya—these all resemble the shape of the gourd.

What on earth, then, is the beauty in the shape of the gourd? What is its special trait? Its demureness, inartificiality and simplicity are born when things are reduced to their original shape. Its qualities are owing not to the core of the shape, but closest to the plane or line. It is the extremity, reached when everything has been taken out, leaving nothing. It is the original nature of form which finally remains on the border of nothingness.

Originally, we developed not the beauty of three-dimensional things but a world of the plane or the line. Three-dimensional beauty is one which is diverse, complicated, massive and concrete. Three-dimensional things can be broken. They change the nature of space into matter. Three dimensionality does not allow room for space, or occasion for silence.

The form of Westerners is like a diamond, multi-faceted and pointed; but the form of the Korean, or for that matter every East Asian, is like the gourd—plain, simple and round. While the beauty of conquering space is a beauty of the form of the West, the Korean beauty of form is one of unifying and harmonizing with space. Our love for the round and abstract form of a gourd may be explained in terms of the fact that by nature we aspire to be one with the nothingness of mother nature in order to annihilate ourselves. Westerners have a tendency to turn a simple shape into a complex one, as when they cut a diamond, while the Koreans transform a complicated shape into a simple one, like a gourd.

It may be the image of the Korean who has no heart left to feel any more suffering after being deprived to the utmost.

Author's note: In *Portrait of France and the French*, André Maurois said, "The English painters idealize their object; the French paint the object as it is, trying to find beauty even in ugliness."

But unlike the English and French, the Korean painters do not idealize or find beauty in ugliness. They eliminate the unnecessary and simplify the object. They attempt to take the essense, hidden behind the form. Oriental, that is, Korean painting, consisting of two dimensions, relies for its effect on empty space which is derived from the secret of restoring form to emptiness.

45. On the Beauty of Color

Depth of color, softly shaded;
Iridescent kingfisher;
Blue sky glimpsed through autumn clouds
As the rain squall passes on;
Or a white cloud, fresh with dew,
Wings its way on high.
But wake! for this is Koryŏ celadon,
This was ours for a thousand years!

THIS is a stanza from Wolt'an's poem, which praises the beautiful color of Koryŏ celadon. Foreign art specialists and Koreans alike bow before Koryŏ celadon. It calls us beyond a simple mood of beauty to a feeling of sublime religious belief. Some foreigners have gone so far as to

---

1.   See page 204 for a complete translation.

exclaim that it points a path to God.

We cannot help but wonder at its mysterious color, not to mention the shape of the pottery. It is a commonplace that in Korea the beauty of color has not been developed. I have mentioned this in the chapter entitled "Are Korean Clothes White?" wherein I have said that the sensitivity to color sprouts forth from the enjoyment of life. Where there is life and joy, there is color; where there is interest in physical things, there is a mind to produce color.

Night and death and tragedy deny and escape from color. Therefore, for the fearful Koreans who have lived in the gloomy history of anguish and restraint, the concept of colors must have been influenced accordingly.

If such is the case, how can we explain the mysterious beauty of the celadon's color which few people have been able to create? Without solving this enigma, one cannot elucidate the relationship between Koreans and the colors they love.

Surely there hasn't been a brilliant color in our life. Starvation for color sometimes resulted in a row of exaggerated and overpowering primary colors, such as vermilion or blue-green in striped Korean clothes or in buildings; in general, however, we have restrained and killed our sensitivity to color.

True, we have shunned bright and stimulating colors, but we have not denied the appreciation of the beauty of colors themselves. Only the nature of color was different.

The complicated subtle blue-green color, as in Koryŏ celadon, and the white color in Yi Dynasty pottery, are the colors which the Koreans have discovered. What do we find, then, in the quality of these colors?

According to a German writer on aesthetics, red and yellow are active colors, somewhat stimulating and strong. But blue-green and violet are passive, cold and lonely. Goethe has defined green as "stimulation in a void." "Yellow always accompanies light." But what the color of blue contains is something shadowy. The color which goes together with shadows acts on the eyes in a manner special and almost inexpressible.

Blue-green is a contradictory color. It is an enigmatic color, born from the unification of two contradictory aspects: stimulation and repose.

Like the high sky and the distant mountains which seem blue, the surface of the blue-green color seems to retreat before our eyes. We enjoy blue-green color because it draws us closer rather than pressing hard to overpower us.

Blue gives us a chilly feeling, reminding us of shade. As Goethe said, blue is a consciousness of nothingness, a consciousness of something remote and afar like God. It is a color like the secretly sobbing soul in the depths of death—a shadow, darkness, silence.

Life in death, eloquence in silence; it is a contradictory color, a color of stimulation in a void.

The blue-green of Koryŏ celadon is attained by sublimating those elements of the blue-green to the maximum. The color is completely buried within the pottery. Although it is a clear color, its depth is closer to the color of the mugwort. But it is not a dark color. Rather, we might say it is a color which attains depth by seeping into the interior, or it is the color of eternity and infinity, an insubstantial color. It is a mysterious color which is hidden while manifesting itself, and is sorrowful while joyful.

This enigmatic color of celadon which appears as if it were about to speak is the color that nobody could create and understand except Koreans.

It is, in a word, an inwardly bruised color. Because we have lived sadly and lonelily with tearful grievances, we have not known such warm, active, bright and flaming colors as red and yellow.

We had to find light in the dark and life in death rather than joy in this world and praise of flaming life. Because ours was a life downtrodden, a tearful fate, we had to replenish our empty hearts with the blue-green color, a color of "void," of nonexistent eternity and empty infinity.

In the midst of agony we were on tiptoe seeking something, as if we were looking up to the sky and out over the sea, not at the rough earth; it must have been the blue-green color of Koryŏ celadon which appeared before our eyes.

A color of inward quietness, of sunken silence.... passive, cool and distant, it draws us and wraps us deep in the shadows. This is the world of Koryŏ celadon, the stimulation in a void. This is the home of the color where the Koreans have rested.

The jade color in the skirts and shoes, the jade hairpin and the color of the Korean fall sky—these are all of the same family.

Koryŏ Celadon

Pak Chong-hwa

Bluish green with subtle lines,
O supple smooth curving,
Like a bodhisattva's shoulders,
Grace and elegance combined.
A swallow spurns the waves
And cleaves the April breeze.
But wake!—for this is Koryŏ celadon,
This was ours for a thousand years.

Depth of color, softly shaded;
Iridescent kingfisher;
Blue sky glimpsed through autumn clouds
As the rain squall passes on;
Or a white cloud, fresh with dew,
Wings its way on high.
But wake!—for this is Koryŏ celadon,
This was ours for a thousand years.

Flagons, pitchers, bowls and dishes,
Ink slabs, censers, incense boxes,
Vases, wine cups, pillows, drums;
They are clay—but they are jade!

Pressed designs of clouds and waves,
Inlaid gems and Seven Treasures,
White cranes standing among flowers,
Buddhist figures, lines of verse:
Work of craftsman and of painter,
Art of sculptor in crude clay.
But wake!—for this is Koryŏ celadon,
This was ours for a thousand years.

Anthology of Korean Poetry, compiled and translated by Peter H. Lee.

46. The Origins of Singing with a Husky Voice

THE teacher played the organ. It was old, and the sound of the pedals on which he trod made more noise than the music itself. Often it made strange sounds when the wind leaked through it. But in spite of it all, the music class in rural schools was the most joyful time. It was most fun when the children in the class started to sing joyfully according to the attendance-list order. Of course, those with good voices would always get the highest marks on the examinations. In order to produce nice, clear, lovely sounds, they tried as hard as possible to imitate the girls. It was an unwritten law in rural schools that the boys sang well insofar as they imitated the girls. On the day before the examination they would eat a raw egg

and drink vinegar in order not to have a husky voice.

But one day, unexpectedly, a husky-voiced lad broke this rule and was praised by the teacher. What he sang with such daring was not the song we learned at school but a classical *sijo* poem or an old melody. Mr. Kurada, the Japanese teacher, heard the song silently with a frightened expression. We thought the song strange as the boy sang it with his husky voice, letting the veins stand out on his neck; but the Japanese teacher seemed to be completely attracted to it.

Henceforth, Mr. Kurada often called upon him to sing *sijo* poems. Basically, the teacher recited the poems in the Japanese manner, but his opinion was that Korean songs were more interesting than the Japanese.

We who thought that good songs had to be sung like a girl could not understand his feelings. After some time had passed, I was able to guess the cogency of his judgment—I mean our teacher, that unknown lover of music.

Korean national music and songs have a different attraction from that found in Western songs. We feel it intuitively, not based on complicated theory. Today in the West the fad for jazz has brought with it the popular and specialized type of singing with a "husky voice." But we had already discovered this hundreds of years ago. In the West, from olden times, the voice qualities were classified as male and female, soprano, mezzo-soprano, bass, baritone and tenor. In Korea we treated them as a whole. Ours was a type of vocalization which could never be defined according to such categories. In order to sing, male and female alike must mouth the secret of the husky voice, murky, rough and shaded.

The sounds Koreans liked were not those that deserve the epithet "silk" but rather "hemp." The texture was thick and irregular; it was at once rough and tender.

This is true not only in our songs, but in the sound of the *kayagŭm* and the Korean drum. A scholar of Korean literature has said that the *kayagŭm* and the Korean drum have reverberations. But I think reverberations can be found in the guitar or Western drum, resonance connecting one note with another. There are no reverberations in the sound of the *kayagŭm* and the Korean drum, but rather the strange feeling of a break between notes which are restrained and cut off from each other. The sound is not transparent but murky, not sliding but rough, as if one were banging on living wood, not hollow wood.

Also, Western songs are methodically sung in accordance with a certain tempo, while Koreans sing according to their breath length.

Western musical notation is strictly defined according to pitch and tempo, but in our music it is everywhere implied. Music is no exception to the scientific taste of Westerners who love to classify insects and calculate numbers.

But what is strange is the fact that the Korean songs, while tinged with sadness, have some fun in them. While Western songs have a different feeling depending on whether they are merry marching songs, laments, or gentle serenades, our songs are not so. They are sad, but behind them they give us joy like a marching air. Actually, Korean songs, while being mournful, become brave marching songs if we sing them quickly. In the West, however good music it may be, it cannot compound contradictory emotions.

As a proof, even in a sad air we often insert such interjections as "good" or "well done" to encourage the performer. Even in laments and wails, somehow the interjection "good" pops out.

In Western music, however, this cannot be done. Even an insensitive, unintellectual person would not exclaim "That's good" upon hearing an air from *Tosca* or Solveg's song. Only we Koreans make such an exception on hearing a dirge.

This paradox, this contradiction, is the voice of our people who have accepted sadness as joy and sublimated laments into gaiety.

How our ancestors sang laments with such passion! We know why they had to sing with a hoarse voice and mixed, shadowy, dull sounds. The reason the sound of the *kayagŭm* and the Korean drum stops the moment it is heard, like a raindrop on the Paulownia leaves, and why such sorrowful songs often produce gaiety rather than tears—one who knows Korean history knows this secret.

47. *Mŏt* and Style

Translator's note: The concept of *mŏt*(멋) in Korean thought is quite important in the discussion of many aspects of Korean life, as will be noted below. The following article attempts to describe the differences between it and "style." For clarity the word has not been translated in this article. The dictionary definitions cover a broad range and include the following: dandyism, smartness, stylishness, tastefulness, elegance, charm, reason, wilfulness. In describing appearances it may often be translated as smart or chic.

IN our language there are various aspects to the word *mŏt*, and it seems that there are few other words which we use with such diversity. At times there are many arguments in intellectual circles on the use of the word *mŏt*. That in itself may be a lack of *mŏt*(멋적은).

People often compare *mŏt* with the Western word "style." If we look in the dictionary, the definition of *mŏt*

209

is a refined and well-formed body or chicness and hand-someness. We cannot have any objection to saying that it is a physical or formal beauty like the word "style." The term *mŏtchangi* (멋장이) does certainly equal the English "dandy." But if we explore carefully the terms *mŏt* and "style" it is clear that they have quite opposite characters. The meaning of "style" is a definite rule with a pattern and a certain form and order.

Originally the meaning of the word "style" came from carving something with an iron pen or stylus.

So we can say that "style" is providing some definite order to chaos and disorder, like the unification of disparate elements within a certain framework. A lack of "style" means the lack of a tendency towards a unifying nature and a definite rule and also the absence of a special form and tendency. "Stylize" means conformity and the fitting to a form. Thus the meaning of "style" is something in vogue, and also regulations and fashion.

But *mŏt* has quite the opposite character to that of "style." Rather, *mŏt* is produced when a definite form or special tendency and a general order and rule have been broken. Let's take a look at such words as "somewhat unbecoming" (a little *mŏt* 멋적다) and "unbecoming" (without *mŏt* 멋없다). Unbecoming means unpolished or unsalty (싱겁다), and that expresses a sense of being tasteless and dried out from the repetition of a rule and traditional conformity.

If one wears a hat crookedly, people look at him and say he tries to use *mŏt* (멋부리다). If he doesn't button all the buttons on his jacket and leaves one undone, we say that this is *mŏt*. People say that it has *mŏt* (멋지다)

210

when they see that rules are not adhered to and when a unified style is lightly ignored. *Mŏt* is when something is outside of formality and when it breaks an order which is set in a framework.

When we see a rather obvious person we say he is a square (a guy with no *mŏt* 멋없는 놈) and when we see something which is too tightly patterned without any feeling of space or openness we say that a sense of *mŏt* (멋대 가리) is lacking. So we can say that *mot* springs from a breakage with and an escape from "style."

Rather than explain it in greater detail, the expression "do as you will" (lit. in accordance with *mŏt* 멋대로) proves this point. When we see self-indulgent acts, we express it by saying "He is playing just as he wishes" (lit. playing in accordance with *mŏt* 멋대로 논다). The sayings which include the expression *mŏt*, such as "You do as you want" and "I do what I want," indicate an action which does not restrain freedom. So we also have the proverb "The Buddhist nun makes love to some guy as she wishes. (멋에 치여 중 서방질 한다)" In addition, when we say *mŏt*, it has the same meaning as joyous.

> *"Chŏnan Samgŏri, ho!*
> *The weeping willow, ho!*
> *It hangs down luxuriantly as it wishes, ho!"*

In this folksong "It hangs down luxuriantly as it wishes," which again uses the expression *mŏt*, means joyfulness and at the same time it also means an emotion emitted according to its own laws.

Mŏt is different from "style" and is a word which indicates freedom rather than restraint, liberation rather than control, and autonomy rather than hegemony. *Mŏt* is an emotion which seeks change from uniformity and freedom from restraint. It is the supreme individual consciousness of the Korean.

In the tradition of Confucianism, which always restrains individual consciousness and the consciousness of freedom, the action of doing as one pleases (멋대로 according to one's *mŏt*) was akin to crime. While we may praise something that has *mŏt*, we are a people who think that to act as one pleases is a great error. Therefore *mŏt* is an emotion which springs from freedom, liberation and self-consciousness. But the reason *mŏt* could only be expressed through writing and singing about nature (風流) is that in a Confucian society the only possible way to pursue *mŏt* and one's own joy was through contact with nature.

It is said that we tried to seek beauty in *mŏt* and tried to live our lives in *mŏt*. If we examine this, we can see that we actually are a people who respect individuality and the freedom of consciousness. We must explain this by saying we could not fully exhibit this tendency due to our unnatural social etiquette and Confucian temporizing even though we wanted to have this free consciousness.

When arrested by regulations and tied to formality, *mŏt* cannot be produced. Rather than saying *mŏt* is "style," we can say that the real meaning of life is in being able to taste momentarily the destruction of a predetermined "style." We can say that the real meaning of *mŏt* is simply in refusing a life chained to rules and a life hidden in the mask of formality so that we can pursue the taste for freedom and the real flavor of things which are hidden.

So if we say that the Westerner derives laws from

freedom, totality from individuality and order from confusion, then can't we say that to the contrary the Koreans desire freedom from law, individuality from totality and confusion from order?

We can also say that the use of the term "do as you want"(멋대로 하라 to do according to one's *mŏt*) to mean "be self-indulgent" is also a Korean tragedy.

48. Breaking the Whip

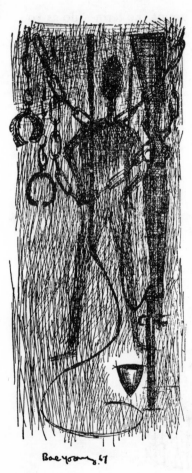

Baeyoung.61

Translator's note: The Korean toy top (팽이) is made to spin by hitting it with a stick on the end of which is tied a piece or pieces of cloth, leather or string, some-what like a cat-o'-nine-tails. A violent striking motion with this whip-like instrument causes the top to spin rapidly. The title of this article in the original might be translated "Breaking the Top Stick."

GREAT Britain is composed of England, Scotland and Ireland, the character of the people varying according to their place of origin. The English are said to be businesslike and the Irish uninteresting. If a Scotsman had his throat cut in a barber shop he is so miserly he would run not to a hospital but to a bloodbank. We can easily see these differences from the following episode:

One day an Englishman invited some guests to his home. One was an Irishman and another a Scotsman. The host told the guests he had fired his maid. He said that there was no other way but to get rid of her because she broke several dishes every day.

The Scotsman's reply was that it would have been appropriate to take the breakage out of her monthly salary. It was very Scottish to calculate the price first in every matter. But the business-like Englishman retorted, "To dismiss her is enough. What would remain if I took money from her salary?"

At that moment, the silly Irish friend answered, "Well, won't it do if you raise her monthly salary and then take out the price of the dishes?"

What would a Korean have said, if he had been present? He would perhaps have said, "Beat her."

It is sad, but this is the way it is. If you beat a Korean he will obey; one who will force a Korean to obey by beating is equally a Korean. Therefore some compare this situation to a top; Koreans, like a top, have to be beaten to get things done. They have lived under aggression, oppression and violence during their history. Actually they harbor some of the elements of a top.

Politicians affirm that they cannot rule this people with gentlemanly ways, democratic methods and compromise. Traffic violators would obey the ordinance if beaten; noisy demonstrations would disappear in one morning if demonstrators were pressed by rifles and swords.

Such argument can develop into the political theory that in our country Western-style democracy simply will not work and benevolent dictatorship is necessary. They say that it won't do to give too much freedom to this people.

But to compare the nature of the Koreans to a top is wrong in all aspects. Would not the Koreans obey if there were no oppression and violence? Are we a people who must have dictators?

In answer to this sort of question, we can put forth proofs that such is not the case.

First, if we analyze the proverb "If you coax someone to do something they won't do it," we can see the character of our people who have tried to live by spontaneous emotions rather than by oppression.

The gist of the Korean emotion is that we do things when we want to do them but, if forced, we won't do them even if we want to. If you don't know this truth, you can't rule the Koreans.

That one must be hit like a top before he will obey is, therefore, nothing but a superficial observation.

Rulers have tried to coax the people, but the people did not listen. Then they used force. The criminality is not in the people for kneeling under violence but in those who enticed them.

Secondly, we often use the expression *shinnanda*(신난다), "self-will." We do things when we enter into their spirit. The word *shin* (신) means a spontaneous pleasure and uncompensated act.

We are a people who can bear any hardship with a feeling of self-will *(shin)* or *shinmyŏng*(신명). Needless to say, beating does not produce such a feeling but extinguishes it. We have been a people who could make use of self-will, but the rulers have always killed it. We did not move because there was nothing to cause self-will, no one to encourage it. We were in a deep sleep. No matter how you beat the people, they will not awaken from that unhappy sleep.

Only when one is able to have self-will in one's own heart can the candle of the East be lit. It is not due to a lack of punishment that we have lived poorly or wandered on a deserted plain. As for the "punishment" (restraint and pressure), we have been beaten for several thousand years.

What we lacked was this freedom and democratic rulers who could evoke this feeling of entering into the spirit of willingness. Those who can rule a people who "if coaxed won't do it" are not the dictators who have the whip to make the tops spin. We have had too many leaders of this kind.

One who knows the Koreans well will first eliminate this coaxing. The leader whom the people will love and follow is one who really understands the people's self-will (신), not one who tries to entice them by saying "do this" or "do that." If you want to rule the Koreans, you must first stop enticing them and break the whip.

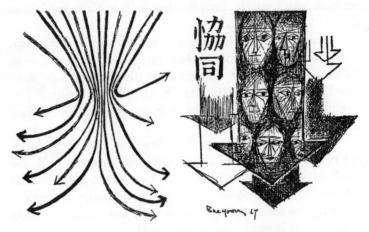

49. On Cooperation

Translator's note: The term *karaejil* (가래질) means the joint action of three men in wielding a shovel. One holds the shovel, while two men, one on each side, assist in the process by pulling the shovel with ropes which have been attached to it. The *kye*(계) is a traditional form of Korean credit union. Individuals band together and put in a certain amount of money monthly. The total is given to each person in turn, which has been decided by drawing lots. It is a ubiquitous system throughout Korea.

THEY say that the more Koreans gather together the weaker they are. In sports, for example, we are superior in individual skills such as weightlifting and the marathon but not in games which need team work. Some say scornfully that with three people, Koreans form factions and a political party.

Judging from our current reality, it is understandable that we lack the cooperative spirit. But can we define it as simply as this? In order to delve into this sort of question we must first discuss the idea of cooperation.

The Chinese character for cooperation(協) is composed of strength(力) put together from various directions with a cross(十). The English word "cooperation" is composed of "co-" plus "operate." So there is more than one way "to gather strength together."

The Western sense of cooperation is exemplified when a bus gets stuck in the mud and everyone gathers together to push it in the same direction. This sort of cooperation might need the strength of one more person, but it doesn't interfere with the effort. The system of cooperation among Koreans is different, however.

Like cooperative shoveling(가래질), it is not a cooperative effort in a given direction, but rather each man pulls in a different direction. One pulls on the right, another on the left, and the third in the center pushes the shovel right in front of him. The directions are all different, and the strength of each pulling and pushing is self-centered. Therefore if the breathing of each is not in harmony, their strength is scattered and the shovel drags its own way.

Perhaps herein lie the secret and the characteristic of Korean cooperation. In other words, the cooperation of the Korean, like that of three men with a shovel, demands a unity of action. One can't pull too much in his own direction because he is strong, nor can one loosen his string because he is weak. It would not be cooperation if one only exhibits his own strength.

Like the men at joint shoveling, the action and the balance of strength centered on each man must be in harmony. With such harmony, they can even dig a canal.

Unlike the cooperation of many getting together and joining their strength to push a carriage, if Korean cooperation is not in unison it becomes an obstacle rather than a help, bringing damage to everyone concerned. In Korean cooperation, breathing is most important. If the rhythm is not harmonious, we cannot gather our strength, and if one man's breathing is not in harmony, the whole balance is broken in this "delicate" cooperation. Then we can say that we have tasted bitter dregs because we attempted to do things without understanding the spirit of joint shoveling in which each plays his individual role and gathers strength with others. It is not that we lack the sense of cooperation, but our method is too delicate.

To speak in more concrete terms, Korean cooperation is not that of the agricultural communes, but cooperation in which individual interest plays an important role. Without self-centered awareness, cooperation will not follow. The prosperity of the community is built while fully maintaining the self-centeredness of each individual.

Let us think about the kye(계) which Koreans like. In the kye many gather together mostly for individual benefit. But the kye, which was organized for individual gain, actually gives benefit to every member.

As is commonly said, there can't be cooperation if it is not a case of a communality of mutual interests. If one reneges on his payments, among the members of the kye the whole unit is broken, as in the case of joint shoveling. The nature of such cooperation is found in farmers' music (두레소리) and everything that begins with the word *ture* (두레)—*turemo*(두레 모 joint planting of rice seedlings), *ture kilssam*(두레 길쌈 joint weaving), and the like. Many gather together to help plant one person's field. Then they gather together again to help plant another's field.

The special group labor system of the Koreans is a product of helping each other in turn according to a set order, like that of getting money from a *kye*. If this kind of direct individual benefit is not involved and if the breathing of the members is not synchronized, then the cooperative effort will be broken. The reason for a lack of cooperation everywhere today lies in the fact that such breathing and self-centeredness have not been permitted. The cooperative system was not built on the individual but instead there was an attempt to gather group strength with uniformity. Hence people were scattered and confusion resulted.

If we look at the ways of cooperation in the villages, such as joint planting of rice, joint weaving and various kinds of *kye*, we see that the nature of cooperation is not foreign to our people. Everyone has been playing an individual game because our kind of cooperation has had no interrelationships and no concern for the individual.

We were defeated during the Japanese invasion of 1592 –8; but how bravely our volunteer "righteous troops" fought in that defeat while our leaders were insufficient and our power was split. And why did our volunteers fight so well with farm implements and sickles while the regular army was so weak and was chased? We know what

Korean joint strength is from this incident.

Korea is strong when, as in the joint shoveling, individual actions from various individuals are joined together. But Korea is weak when the individual is forced to exert himself in a joint action through social or national conformity.

If the breathing and rhythm don't match, the more Koreans who gather together the more divided they become. Because such a democratic people have been ruled by such dictatorial methods, their society was inevitably fragmented and destroyed.

We should not forget the Korean ideal: "The hands and feet must be coordinated even in robbery."

Author's note: We can presume how the people were united and cooperated in ancient Korea from the groups of rural people called the *Hyangdo* (鄉徒) and the *Kye* (契). Dr. Lee Sang-ok has written in his *History of Korea:*

"The *Hyangdo* was generally a low-class group of neighbors gathered together. A large one consisted of one hundred members and a small one of eight or nine. They had fun and drank together in sequence every month and if someone died who was a relative of someone in the group, the friends prepared clothes for mourning and provided the coffin. They helped carry the torches and sometimes supplied food. They sometimes even made the tomb and mourned as well. The *Hyangdo* became pallbearers. This was very popular and a spirit of unity was fostered especially when it was essential during the busy agricultural seasons. They thought it natural to assist each other by bringing all their strength to bear collectively at those times. If there was a good harvest, they became more genial and kind, and they then could even think of luxuries."

Conclusion

50. Standing on the Hill of the Shrine of the Guardian Spirits

ON a quiet lane on a lonely hill, one always confronts a shrine to the local guardian spirits. The faces of the spirits on the pillars, weathered by rain and wind, stand silently, their feet buried in a heap of cold pebbles. Only a trace remains of the characters written in India ink, "Great General of All Under Heaven" and "The Female General of the Underworld."

How much wind, how many clouds, stars and mournful desires have passed by this pair of wooden statues? Here is the rustic but infinitely secret altar of the Koreans. This is the place where every passer-by stopped and prayed for the fulfilment of his wishes, unheard by anyone else.

"Please grant me a son," "Please give me three meals a day," "Please let my husband who has gone to market return safely," "Please let the grain ripen fruitfully in the fields," "Please let him love me" and "Please let me sleep"— they had no other recourse but to pray and beg the statues of the guardian spirits to grant their wishes, large and small.

These people have been especially lachrymose and full of grievances, but their altar where they knelt and prayed was so modest. There were no candles, no incense, and no ceremony and music. Because they had nothing, they had nothing to offer. There was nothing for them to do but to pick up muddy stones rolling on the road and throw them as offerings at the feet of the statues.

But we know the pebbles they offered with rough and hard hands were steeped in so many stories and deep prayers.

Who has answered their prayers? Was there anyone but the statues, which they encountered on their comings and goings, to listen to their wishes?

Theirs was an altar without the sound of a pipe organ and without glittering, brilliant mosaic windows. The poor spirit altar and the lonely wooden statues—weren't these the history and life of these people? They had no way to express their desires, no way to realize their dreams. Look at the people bowing on the hill of the spirit shrine, throwing stones as offerings and clasping their hands in silence!

Their eyes are resigned, their necks tired, their tight lips expressionless; but in their hearts still burns the mind's candle—hence they cannot give up their one wish.

Standing on the hill of the spirit shrine what must we pray for today? What have been the wishes of this earth, of the father, his son and his grandson? They still throw stones. They still clasp their hands. The wooden statues stand with their thousand-year-old faces. When we kneel before the spirit shrine it seems we can understand our sorrows, our fate and our hopes.

These are not luxurious prayers. They only ask for no more trouble for the weak, the poor, the unhappy and the suffering. Before this ruined altar there is no change in the content of their lives from a thousand years ago and a thousand years later ... a people who could not even say they were alive, a people who starved for love and thirsted after peace, a people who could not even feel anger against those who exploited and trampled on them leaving them only a ruined life. If they were asked to go, they went; if they were asked to stay, they stayed.

Neither foreigners nor countrymen have gently touched their wounds with loving hands. They have lived single-handedly, consoling their grievances as if they were a secret, and enduring the hardships with submission; but there still remains the unhappiness they have to bear. For those who could not keep their feet on the ground, even a withdrawal from public life in an attempt to seek a hermit's life in nature is not permitted. The world has become a place where they cannot live a life of their own as they are or as they deserve.

Now they are compelled to eat dumplings made from imported wheat and find happiness in fingernails manicured with polish rather than with the balsam flower. The world has become a difficult place to cherish even in their hearts buried in the earth. The time has come for them either to stand up or be destroyed. The time has come to light the fire in the hearts of this people who have lived a lukewarm hesitating life. For tomorrow we must stop a tearful prayer to the guardian spirits, we must put an end to the life of shame. A new Korea will be born the day this four thousand-year-old hermit looks squarely at his own wounds and is rejuvenated and gets fiercely angry at his own shameful history.

Until we build a new bridge over the history of our country, which like a single wooden span has been broken countless times, the pebbles at the spirit shrine will be heaped higher and higher.